Morning THOUGHTS

CHRISTOPHER WILLS

ISBN 978-1-0980-5387-1 (paperback)
ISBN 978-1-0980-5388-8 (digital)

Christian Faith Publishing, Inc.
832 Park Avenue
Meadville, PA 16335
www.christianfaithpublishing.com

Printed in the United States of America

INTRODUCTION

I wanted to do this introduction because what you're about to read are some of my daily thoughts. It details all of my life, from peaks I've been able to reach to valleys I've plummeted to. Throughout the journey, I received blessings and endured losses all along the way. Why would I do this? Why would I put my life in the spotlight for everyone to see? Great questions, I'm glad you asked…here's why. I want people to know that they're not alone in their struggle. I have decided to be transparent so that someone reading this can feel better as they deal with their own story. I hope to encourage; uplift; give a different perspective and maybe open eyes, hearts, and minds. I want to draw people close (or closer) to their higher power. However, you choose to address them. I tend to leave no stone unturned so we will be bonding a lot as you read.

During this read, you will learn a lot about me. So again, hi, my name is Chris…pleasure to meet you… I hope you enjoy this book. I pray that you're able to take something away from one or all of the messages and that they put a smile on your face, joy in your heart, relief in your mind, and maybe even a new or renewed faith in He who gives us all. I thank you and I hope you enjoy!

CHAPTER 1

A song was once written that said it
best... "You Are Not Alone."

At a young age, I would put myself down first before anyone else got the opportunity to. It became a defense mechanism to keep me shielded from potential hurt. In the process, I convinced myself that I was lesser than. My life lessons at that time taught me that to open up would result in rejection and hurt feelings and who wants to volunteer for that roller-coaster ride? So I did what most people do when they're afraid of being hurt, I isolated myself. Even around groups of people, I always felt that, at the end of the day, I was alone, and if that's the case, I have to do what's best for me as I see fit... thank God that's no longer that skin I'm in...but that's not the case for many. We live in a society where isolation is the preferred means of existence. Everyone yearns to be with others but predominantly strive to keep to themselves, the very infrastructure of social media... hopefully, you get that double entendre, but if not, it will click in later... I digress...

Proverbs 18:1 (NIV) says, "A man who isolates himself seeks his own desires; He rages against all wise judgment." The greatest trick the devil ever performed was convincing the world that he doesn't exist...followed 1 Pet. 5:8. In a world constructed to keep everyone apart, it's easier for the predator to stalk its prey. I cannot allow myself to fall victim to the systemic trap that God's adversary has set before my blessings. God never intended for any of us to be alone... just ask Adam... (Gen. 2:18). God gave me my body and provided me with a body... (1 Cor. 12:12–27). He provided me with people with whom I can work with collectively for all of our betterment. He gives me a family. He gives me spiritual edification, listening ears, encouraging fellowship, shoulders to cry on, and then charges me to perform the same duties for those around me when they need the same. Iron truly sharpens iron...sidenote, understand that that's one of the most painful processes with the most miraculous results, which is a discussion for another time.

Bottom line, for me, the worst thing I can do is stay to myself. It is self-destructive to determine that isolation is the best decision for me. Now I'm in no way saying that quiet time or time of meditation when I'm alone are not necessary...even Jesus needed to be still and be to himself, but those moments are not meant to be a charted life course. If isolation leads to me pursuing my own selfish desires, how can any good come of it? Well, that's the point...

You are not alone...the devil just wants to convince you that you are. Know the difference and flee from that existence. I know all too well what that life looks like, feels like, tastes like, and quite honestly, it's no life at all...but why would it be when the creator of that path's intention is to take life, not nurture it. Stop isolating yourself and let love in. I promise when you begin to look for real love as defined in 1 Cor. 13:4–8, you will open your eyes to a whole new world and the blessings that God intended for you will be there...

Have a blessed day on and in purpose!

CHAPTER 2

*Some of our greatest battles are the ones we
made a conscious decision not to fight.*

I am learning that I don't need to respond to everything. I am finding discernment in knowing when and where to do what and why. Truly there is a peace of mind that can be found in simply picking my battles. Some things are just NOT worth it. Even Jesus walked away from a few unnecessary situations. Bruce Lee referred to it as "the art of fighting without fighting."

Some people look for confrontation. It's the only way that they can express themselves and make themselves feel special, more powerful, bigger, badder, etc. In their minds, they feel that making someone feel small makes them feel better about themselves. It has become a defense mechanism to avoid having to address their own inequities.

Knowing that, why would I allow that to cause a transference of energy on my part? Now don't get me wrong, I have very strong and intense "Peter" tendencies when provoked, so I of all people, I know how hard it is to take the higher path and turn the other cheek. But when I understand the nature of a thing, why place unfair expectations upon it? One of the most powerful quotes someone shared with me goes "You cannot ask a sick person a well question and expect a well answer." I have to remind myself of that daily and govern my actions and interactions accordingly.

But the thing that always humbles me is knowing that God has to do the same thing with me on a regular basis. Not that I pick fights with Him. Then again, maybe I do, but that He asked me a "well" question, and I've given Him a "sick" answer. He has remained patient, loving, graceful, and merciful with me, in spite of me and so who am I to walk around feeling as though I am not obligated to do the very same?

No one has power over how I feel unless I choose to give them said power. Today I strive to pick my battles better and discern more when I need to respond and or act, if at all.

Have a blessed day on and in purpose!!!

CHAPTER 3

*I will never be perfect, but I will
die striving for perfection.*

I've been living with a pinched nerve in my lower back for almost two years now. It affects my entire left leg, and one of my toes has remained numb. At one point, I wasn't even sure how I was going to make it from my car to my desk at work. The pain was unbearable and impacted my everyday activities. I went to the doctor's, it was diagnosed, and they then prescribed medication. It worked well for a little while and made the pain tolerable, but then the pain came back with a vengeance! I went back to the doctor, she changed my medication (which works *wonders*!!!) and it was then that she arranged PT. It was at physical therapy that I learned exercises that will help make my condition copable. It was explained that my pinch nerve will never go away…but that I could do things to make it easier to deal with.

Now I could've just popped the pills and expect that to be enough because the pain reduced dramatically after I started taking it, but I would not have been doing everything within my power to make my situation as the best situation possible. I put in the work, I still do my exercises and stretches. I watch what I lift and, more importantly, how I lift. I also try to stay active. The pain is still there, there were not lying when they said it would not go away, but I continue to do what's necessary so hopefully one day, I will wake up and the pain won't be there.

I'm sorry...where am I going with this??? Oh! My bad...ok, here it is... I am far from perfect. I make mistakes, bad decisions, and I've lost count of how many times I've said I'm sorry. Changing my path in no way changes the fact that I remain a sinner overflowing with imperfect tendencies...but I refuse to let that be my end all be all. I refuse to accept that *that's* all I'll ever be. Yeah, God knows what's in my heart, but I'm not comfortable with the measure of my existence being contingent on something internal that was never personified externally. I have to put in the work. I have to do the things that make my situation the best situation possible. Much like my pinched nerve, my sinful inclinations will always be there, however, they choose to attempt to make themselves manifest. But I will not wimp out and accept them nor expect other things to be the fix for the things I need to implement in my life to make my walk worth living, no pun intended. I will continue to do whatever is necessary to make my situation the best situation possible or die trying... As someone so eloquently said to me this week, "When I see God, I hope to hear 'Well done' and not "Well...'."

Have a blessed day on and in purpose!!!

CHAPTER 4

It's not you, it's me!

I'm learning now, more than ever, that the process is simple, it's me wanting to do the process my way that complicates things. My focus needs to be on my heavenly father and everything else will fall into place. Easier said than done. When I reflect on my life and look at the places where I fell, stumbled, made huge mistakes, etc…one of the constant and consistent variables to those situations was that I was trying to do things on my own…void of God. Whenever I take God out of the equation, the math never adds up correctly.

Matthew 6:33 has been a mantra of mine for a few years now and also one of the hardest scriptures for me to follow because I have to surrender control of my life. I have to relinquish authority over who I am to Him in a time when I am the most lost and unsure what to do. The scripture is simple in it's context, but I fear what it entails because there are no guarantees. I am promised but it's my human inclination to want immediate results after I say "Amen." There are no confirmed absolutes, there's just faith and hope. Most times, it's very hard to see those things as physically tangible until after they've been made manifest. That's why I find it beneficial to read the entire chapter to remind myself who I serve and why I have nothing to fear. Not to say that I won't find myself confronted with situations or "stresses," but it comforts me that when I focus on Him, it's clear that worrying is a waste of time and energy because everything is going to happen regardless.

When I begin to think about how to fix this, I immediately picture myself standing in front of that tree with the snake talking to me. I remember who I made lord of my life and why I need to give it over to Him, exercising faith that He will provide an answer, whatever it may be.

Sometimes we try to do things on our own because we fear that the answer may be no. But there's a reason and purpose to everything. It's not for us to question him but to have faith, knowing that he knows what's best for us. Sometimes we overlook the fact that *no* does not always mean "never." It could mean "just not right now." But that's a whole other conversation. No one ever said life was easy, but it does get easier to deal with when you just follow the map and strive to get to your purpose and destination in life.

Have a blessed day on and in purpose!

CHAPTER 5

When I think of love...

When I made Jesus Lord of my life, shortly thereafter, I lost my relationship with my mother and father. The religion they followed deemed it necessary to sever ties with me because of my newfound beliefs. I was hurt, lost, and outraged. How could my parents just discard me like that? How could they turn their backs on me when I still need them in my life? I've never been without them in my life, like *ever*! Where's God in that? I fought it tooth and nail, from local discussions with elders to their religion's Supreme Court in Bethel, all to no avail. No sound biblical explanation was ever given, and no rational answer was ever expressed. I sent letters, left messages, and drove past their house hoping they would be outside just so I could see them. Nothing.

Three years went by, I got a call from my brother. He said, "Your mother's in the hospital. She has brain and pancreatic cancer." My world stopped and shook at the same time. It was evening and they were still trying to get her situated. I told my brother I would be there in the morning and to let those who needed to be advised know that I coming. "I'm not asking for permission, I'm coming."

I was blessed to spend time with my mother during her last ten days on this earth. I was able to hold her hand, laugh with her, be in her space, and just absorb her energy. It was like the last three years never occurred. In her last moments, I will never forget looking up and seeing my whole family standing around her, holding hands as she prayed and recited her favorite scriptures. She left this earth faithful to her God. That's love.

I find peace knowing that she never loved me less, she just loved God more! She was willing to sacrifice anything and everything to maintain that love, just as Jesus died for me. I could never be mad at her for falling in love with God. It's what we're all called to do. Love is never selfish. That was my sin, not hers. I pray that we all learn to love like my mother loved. I pray that we find love and that we be loved to the extent that God was loved by mother.

R.I.H. Mom! Know that I will *always* love you!

Have a blessed day on and in purpose!

*I can no longer be afraid to stand up for
myself for fear of how it will affect others.*

My teenage years were filled with rejection and ridicule. Consequently, I developed very low self-esteem and an addiction to outside valida-tion. When I met people who actually wanted to be in my space, I would do whatever it took to keep them there, sacrificing myself in the process. I figured that as long as I made them happy, they would stay. I would not argue when they did something I didn't like for fear that if I confronted them, they would leave. Many had after getting what they wanted. It became a vicious cycle that lead to years of pain, bad decisions, and regret. It then took years of self-assessment, reflection, and therapy to become far removed from the young man I once was.

Thank God for being there even when I wasn't at that point in my life where I was ready to acknowledge His presence in it…

Isaiah 41:10 is His promise to us. Whether we put weight into it or not, He never breaks a promise…but I digress…

Two things I learned in this process that govern my actions to this day in my life…well three…

1. God is always there for me, and all He wants for me is to know who He is and that He wants nothing but the best

for me, and sometimes I go through things so that I can get out of my own way in order to see Him more clearly. It all starts with Him. And when I put Him first, everything else begins to fall into place, and I can begin to distinguish the forest from the trees.

2. I will never meet anyone's expectations, unless their expectations are in line with God's will, specifically His will for my life. I will never be able to make anyone happy if their happiness is dependent on things that are not of God. I will never be able to meet those expectations because they're not purposed for me. I also know that it is a waste of time to place expectations on others that are not of God. Sometimes the change simply begins with me not expecting the change to occur in others…but that's a conversation for another time…

3. I am worthy of having persons, places, and things in my life that love me for who I am, not who I feel I need to be to maintain them in my life. I now love myself enough to know that not everyone is meant to be in my life, and those that will, do so because they can accept me at my highs and lows, my good days and my bad days. Where as in the past, I would be hesitant to express myself for fear of how it would be received or fear of making someone unhappy or fear of that person leaving my life, now I know the power, freedom, and peace of mind in respectfully articulating my feelings so that those around me are aware of where I am at how I am feeling, and having the dialogue necessary to move forward productively, even if that moving forward means that I'm moving over here and they're moving over there.

I am no longer afraid of losing someone because God promised me that He will always be with me. I learned that so many things that I had in my space were never meant to be there and me keeping them there for selfish reasons did more harm than good…a whole new perspective on the phrase "Let go and let

God." Today I know I need to stand in faith, stand in love, stand in discernment, but most importantly, today I know that I simply need to *stand*!

Have a blessed day on and in purpose!

CHAPTER 7

My response is my responsibility.

I heard these words last week and they definitely resonated with me, but looking at them further, do I really implement the meaning behind the words?

I can be quick to look at what a person did that I felt was the catalyst to my response, be it word or deed. I can even justify my actions simply by saying, "but they did this or that." But at the end of the day, I will have to render an account for the things I chose to do, and there will be no excuses accepted.

People are just evil these days. They don't even realize it. False sense of self-entitlement has crept into every facet of life. People say and do whatever they please with little to no regard of the consequences. They make it very hard to be responsible. Very, very, very hard! My Alley McBeal moments be *serious*! Some of you know what that's about...lol... I digress...

None of this changes the charge that I've been given. Regardless of what anyone does or why they do it, my response is my responsibility. In that statement is the key. When I focus on my life, getting it together and aligning it with God's will, I have less time worry about what others are doing or why. It's when I focus on being the best me I can be that I see clearly how to be the best me for others. Not my will but His be done.

In these days, it has become much harder to do. That does not means that it can't be done. Just more confirmation that it's the combination of faith and works that makes each day a victory simply because He got us through it.

Have a blessed day on and in purpose!

CHAPTER 8

My level of happiness is determined by
the things I pursue to achieve it.

Some of the richest people are the very persons who go to sleep every night depressed. The people with the most possessions are some of the unhappiest people walking around. There's more to happiness than what you have. True happiness stems from who you are. If I don't know who I am, if I have no concept of who or what to believe in, how can I ever find true happiness? Observation. Many people try to use material possessions or even people to fill a void within themselves that only knowledge of self can fill.

I modeled clothes for a little over ten years. It was a life that no one could have convinced me I would have lived. It opened my eyes to a world I thought I'd never see. But my passion for it was fueled by an addiction to outside validation. I craved having hundreds, thousands of people looking at me and wanting to be me wanting to be with me, but then when I got off the stage, I reverted back to the person that no one paid attention to or wanted to be around. At the end of the day, I was still me. I was still very unhappy with my life.

Then I began to learn who I was. God put the right persons, places, and things in my space, and I began to love me for me. I began to accept me for who I am, the good, the bad, and the very ugly. I began to see that I did have something to offer this world and that I was worthy of so many things, love, respect, genuine time, and attention. I learned that happiness starts from within. Once I had the revelation that my happiness did not depend of the attention of others, it changed my whole outlook on outside validation. Whereas I used to yearn for it, I felt I couldn't live without, I endured a plethora of drama to have it, now it became a turn off because the actions behind it rarely prove to be genuine. I was making myself happy so it changed how I looked at others trying to make me happy. Either people were coming into my space to enhance or their presence was not needed. You either add to or you're immediately subtracted from my space these days.

I learned that when I am happy within myself, happiness from outside sources is no longer needed…it's wanted and when something is wanted, I can go with or without it, and that's a freedom that I had overlooked for so long.

If you're unhappy…money won't do it. If happiness eludes you, it will not be found in material possessions. If you yearn for true happiness, you will not find it in that person. Those persons, places, and things can only enhance the happiness you already possess within. They will *never* fill that void. And that void will never truly be filled until you have that relationship with your higher power. Even with knowledge of self, I wasn't truly happy. I was just happier because I was no longer making decisions that were self-defeating and self-destroying. I can truly say that I am happy now because I know my knowledge of self includes a knowledge and relationship with He who created me. God is the true void filler and the focal point to all things me. I cannot know who I really am without God, and I will never become who I was destined to be without accepting Him in my life and surrendering to Him.

My life makes sense now. Yes, it's a constant struggle. Each day presents its own obstacles and trials, but knowing I have God and thus when I look at everything around me, I can see Him in it…how can I be anything but happy?! There's not one material possession that can equate the happiness that God has provided me…and my prayer is that you find the very same happiness for your life and those who are in it…

Have a blessed day on and in purpose!

CHAPTER 9

The only way that someone can change my
mood or affect my energy is if I allow them to.

I cannot let unworthy people have worthy privileges. If they get them, then I have no one to blame but myself. When I read about Job, I look at how he handled his friends and his wife. I am humbled. Here he had just lost everything—his children, his property, his wealth, and even his health. All the while, everyone around him is telling him to curse God. Bottom line, he was hurting outside and in. and the persons put in his space are of no help whatsoever. But at no time did he allow any of those things to affect his energy, change his spirit, or distract him from his focus and faith in God. He never lashed out, although he would have been justified. I'm praying for forgiveness now. I know what my reaction would've been…but I digress…

So many times we allow people to change who we are and how we feel. We give them that power but then complain about what they do with it when it was never theirs to have to begin with, nor was it ours to give to them. A lot of times, it's people who don't even matter or that we don't even know… I see people all the time yelling at the top of their lungs in their cars because another driver did something they didn't like. I've also seen that other driver go on about their day while the first driver's day is ruined. I'm sorry but that's crazy to me. You still get to your destination, no one is hurt…life goes on doesn't it? So, why would someone allow a total stranger to take them out-side of 329 themselves and affect them on such a grand scale?

The only person worthy of changing my spirit is God. Other than that, I'm good. To give people power over my mood is like giv-ing a gun to a child. It's a risky move. At the end of the day, if Job was able do it in the circumstances he was in, I have absolutely no excuse. Today I strive to give the power to He who is worthy and will never misuse it in my life.

Have a blessed day on and in purpose!

CHAPTER 10

Sometimes I don't see the blessing because,
while I'm looking for it to come, I overlook
the fact that it's already there.

I like things my way. Who doesn't? I have such a grand layout of how I want my life to be—the look, the texture, the feel, etc. When I pray for something, it's my natural inclination to foresee how that prayer will come to fruition. I've already played it out in my head and wait for what I envisioned to become reality. So when it doesn't, I'm vexed. Why, God, why? Here's why. Want to make God laugh? Tell Him your plans for your life.

It is impossible for me to think like God so why would I even entertain the concept of being able to see how His blessing will come? Why do I do that to myself? I am learning that when I focus on my faith in Him and His will for my life, I can clearly see that many of the things that I've been praying for are already present in my life and working as I requested. It's simply because it didn't come in the package I wanted it to and thus I paid it no mind. I am blessed beyond measure, but I take many of my blessings for granted because they didn't appear in the manner that I would have preferred. Bottom line, I needed to get over myself and get out of my own way if I was ever going to let go and let God...such a silly little mortal I am.

None of us are promised tomorrow (Prov. 27:1, Jas. 4:13–15) so do not spend today taking things for granted. You are blessed beyond measure, whether your blessings came the way you wanted them to or not. So much can easily be taken away in the blink of an eye so hold tight to your blessings. Say thank you for the roof over your head, the clothes on your back, the food you digest, the car you drive, the job you drive it to, and the person you come home to if you're blessed to have them. Be thankful for everything that God has given you because you never know. Say thank you and move in thankfulness, understanding that we're not worthy of anything. By His grace, He blesses us with everything! You cannot have what you want until you want what you have.

Have a blessed day on and in purpose!

CHAPTER 11

My God is an on-time God...not
an ON MY TIME God...

There are times when I look at my life and become a little distraught at the fact that I am almost halfway through it and just getting started in so many ways. Everything happens for a reason. Everything! Yes, I've been running from so much for so long, I can admit that and take responsibility for the time lost and or wasted. But I can also say that I've learned so much from my Forest Gump marathon. Much like him, I stopped at one point and said, "I'm going home now." I've been doing just that—coming home. I "came home" to accept my purpose and embrace my passion and everything that comes with it, confirming how much God loves me. I was coming home to family and friends who have been there all along. I can now see who sent them to me.

So, in essence, I look at my life from a perspective of purpose and understanding that it's not my will, but His. Just like the God I serve, I'm right on schedule. My life is just that, mine. My blessings aren't just starting, I've been blessed all along. I was supposed to be gone a long time ago from car crashes, health conditions, attempted suicide, and even a bullet, but thanks to God, I am still here. I realize that I can lose sight of how amazing God's purpose in my life is when I begin to compare my blessing with others. Their blessings are theirs to praise. I will do the same for mine, knowing that they have been tailor made for me. Today I acknowledge that I am not late in "getting it," rather God is right on time in "giving it."

Have a blessed day on and in purpose!

CHAPTER 12

Growing up, there were times when I would have to defend myself. It didn't go so well. After taking several L's, I began to seek advice so that if I was faced with those circumstances again, I would have more chance of prevailing. I will never forget one of the main lessons I was taught, "Stay on your feet! Never let them get you on the ground!"

I had learned from experience that nine times out of ten, if my opponent got me on the ground, the fight was not only harder to win, but pretty much over. There was the propensity for others to join in. I took that point to heart and incorporated it in my fighting strategy. I learned not only to defend myself, but to do so in a way that I would come out strategically on top. I still fight today, it's just not physically as much as it is mentally, emotionally, and spiritually. That rule still applies.

Stay on your feet! Never let them get you on the ground!

I had to fight some big dudes in my youth, literal David vs. Goliath scenarios, and I had to think more than I had to act. I couldn't stand toe to toe with those dudes so I had to be smarter than them and move faster than them. I had to think ahead and be prepared for what was coming for me. Today is the same, I'm fighting some big demons, both internally and externally...same scenarios, but what I can lose is far greater than just a fight. I have to be smarter. I have to be faster... I have to be ready and prepared for what's coming for me. I have to be equipped (Eph. 6:10–18).

It's not enough for me to say "God help me" and go back to business as usual. I can't go to a job interview with nothing and say, "Give me a job" and expect an employer to go, "Okay, sure!" I can't go to a dealer with no money, no pay stubs or collateral and say, "Give me a car" and expect them to say, "Here you go!" I must do my part to be ready. Just like I learned to defend myself for those fights back then, I must learn how to defend myself for the fights I encounter in my life today. With that, I say I am *nothing* without God! He is my trainer from now until I leave this earth and train with Him in person.

I pray that we're all getting ready today for the fights we will encounter in our lives, accepting that there's no better teacher than my Lord and Savior.

Have a blessed day on and in purpose!

CHAPTER *13*

I am hurting…there, I said it…and
that's where the healing begins…

I have endured a lot of pain in my life, from mental and verbal abuse as a child to emotional hurts as a teenager and to even deeper scars inflicted as a man. I attempted suicide because I thought that was the only way out. I was diagnosed with a blood disorder and given three years to live. I've been robbed at gunpoint. I've been shot. I've experienced emotional hurts that would have crippled most for life. For that matter, I realized that I've been crippled for most of mine.

I've had to watch those I hold dear deal with the damage I caused. I've been on the receiving end of some of the most hurtful words that could ever be uttered, leaving irreparable damage and some of the most horrid, permanent scars. I've been afraid to be open up and absolutely terrified to love for the majority of my tenure here on this earth. Despite all of that, I can say, "I'm still here." I have survived and overcome the very things that could have ended me, but I also have to be careful not to ignore the lasting effects while I'm still here. That's where I've fallen short.

I realized that I've moved on from a lot, but I have not healed from most of it because there are so many things in my life that I was so happy to get away from and survive that I never wanted to revisit those persons, places, and things again. In doing that, I never process those things so they never healed. They kept growing and nurturing into their own demons. I definitely began to realize this when the next brick was added on the wall of my life. It used to take a couple of bricks before I noticed the weight increase. Now I'm feeling every brick being placed.

It's a humbling realization and a scary revelation at the same time. I have to accept that I am human. I forget that. I'm so busy telling myself, "This too shall pass," not understanding that after a tornado passes, it leaves destruction in it's aftermath that must be cleaned up and rebuilt. I have to talk about what I've gone through so that I am better equipped to handle what I'm going through so that with God's help, I can get through! We have to communicate. We have to talk, more importantly, we've got to pray...and not the "give us this day our daily bread" prayer, not saying I have anything against that prayer, but the "Father, I'm dying inside, and I'm struggling to do your will prayer. The God, I feel less than worthy, I feel inferior. I feel like it's a waste of time for me to still be on this earth prayer." The statement of facts that makes you have the ugly cry face. The real in-your-face prayers with God! Then we have to open up to those close to us. We can't keep things bottled up. It will come out... by choice or by force.

Today I can say, "I'm hurt. I'm hurting. I need healing. I need you, God!"

Have a blessed day on and in purpose!

CHAPTER 14

We all grieve. Some just have more
to grieve about than others.

A person could look at me and never have the slightest inkling of what I'm dealing with, the demons I'm fighting, the weight that sits constantly on my shoulders, or the health conditions I have to deal with every day. They see a jovial man who loves life and the pursuit of it. They automatically assume that there can't be anything negative going on because I look happy...no statement. It could be further from the truth. When we watch a duck as it smoothly across a pond, we rarely see, if ever, their effort of paddling beneath the water...

This week alone I was struggling with the fact that Weds was my mother's birthday and for almost 3 years now, she has not been here. I am so thankful that she's in a much better place and now having a realization of who her heavenly Father really is, but I miss her presence here on earth. On top of that, 3 years prior to that, she was void in my life due to circumstances beyond my control. Every day I grapple with the what ifs and the whys even the why Gods... During these times as I'm getting more in tuned and open with my feelings, and all the while direct reminders pimp smack me in my face, I find myself feeling like I'm back at square one. I say all that to say that most people around me were oblivious to what was going on because I came to work. I did my job and carried on with my day, not faking in any way because if anyone had asked me, I would have had no issues telling them, but striving to move in the light of God's love, mercy, grace, wisdom, and power.

This is just one of the plethora of battles I fight every day that God sees fit to open my eyes for another day. As much as I'm confidently willing to put my war stories up against anyone else's, I also know that with as much that I contend with, there are people around me who struggle with so much more, but I will never see by just looking at them. So recognize that kind word you utter to that complete stranger walking past you may be the words that encourages them to fight for one more day because they were on their way to end their life. That kind gesture that you extend to that person who may not even say thank you may be the reassurance that they needed to have just a small glimmer of hope in humanity. That smile or wave you give to someone may actually be the only light from God that they'll see. Who are you to deprive them of that? You never know what someone is going through so never pass up the opportunity to show someone how good God has been to you because there is a lot of doubt behind most of the smiles you view 491 and a whole lot of lack of faith behind the words "I'm good…" Be the light because there are more people dwelling in darkness than meets the eye.

Have a blessed day on and in purpose!

CHAPTER 15

My focus is no longer changing someone's
mind. My focus is being a light.

Back in the day, I *had* to win someone over. I had to win. Even if I was wrong, you could not change my mind. I would fight until I had nothing left. I would have been a chief commander in the Inquisition. It was serious! Thank God for growth and change. These days, I'm about information and dialogue. I'm no longer trying to convert a person I'm conversing with, just trying to have an open exchange of viewpoints. At the end of the day, we may never agree, but I guarantee we're both, whoever I'm engaged in the conversation with, going to leave the discussion with new information and added insight on the topic—or at least I will.

The problem is we no longer talk about things. Everyone is so easily offended. If something sounds like something we're not gonna like, we'd rather shut down the whole conversation. This is counterproductive on so many levels and a time bomb waiting to go off. The truth is not offensive, and a person's opinion is nothing more than that. I find it fascinating how people express their opinion on a daily basis with little to no concern of how it affects others, but then become so irritated when someone responds to their statements. Whether it's 45 or your local FB troll…people are fine until met with opposition.

Today, I can have dialogue with anyone about anything and at the end of the day, it matters not that they're converted at the end, what matters is that I try my utmost to disseminate factual information to those I am engaged in discussions with. I also make it a point to listen intently to what someone is saying not just so that I can gain insight and information that I may not have had before, but so that I can respond properly and with the right understanding of what was said. I find myself learning more than the person I may have attempted to educate and that makes me more knowledgeable going into the next conversation, and knowledge is truly power.

We've got to start talking more. Even more important than that, we've got to start listening! God, in His wisdom, gave us two ears and one mouth for a reason.

Have a blessed day on and in purpose!

CHAPTER 16

I may not be where I want to be, but I've
come so far from where I've been.

This year will make 6 years that I've been sober. It's all still new to be because for thirty-two years of my life, I was a functional alcoholic. Those who've known me long enough remember my days of consumption, partying, etc. Many a story can be told, both good and bad. Last night, I reflected on the person I was versus who I am now. It wasn't a pity party or a woe-is-me experience. A lot of amazing things happened during those years, but even more amazing and significant things are happening now in my life… THAT I can *actually* remember! LOL!

I learned that although the conviction is immediate, the process isn't. I was in the Chemical Recovery Ministry of my church for a minute. It took some time to understand why I was doing what I had been doing for so long. There was a lot of acknowledgment, denial, repentance, a plethora of revelations, and then a firm resolve to never be that person again. It also takes time for others to see the change in you because they're so used to you being who you were. My friends, who have seen my transition, can attest to that. It took a minute for most to see that I was serious this time because I had quit soooo many times before. Now when I go out, people say it before I can, which is crazy to me. We all laugh about it, but it's a testimony to change and true conviction in said change. I am a happy member of the Fruit Punch Crew 4 Life... LOL!

Now, let the record state that I have nothing against anyone having a drink, in moderation... I mean Jesus did turn water into wine...his... But, for me, I vowed never to touch another drop of alcohol because of what it represents in my life. It is a reminder of who I am without God. It is a reminder of the decisions I make in my life void acknowledgement of God's will for it. It is a reminder of how I cope and attempt to find escape without looking to He who holds all answers. It reminds me that I am *nothing* without God.

Everyone has something that they need to move on and move forward from. We all need to start making the changes that best fits our lives. We all need to grow, make better decisions, and want more for our lives when the time is right for us to do so or when life dictates that those things be done. The *if* and *when* is entirely up to every individual on the planet.

Today I reflect and can assess all aspects of the person I was— the good, the bad, and the ugly. Honestly, I can still make that assessment but I fully acknowledge that where I am now is nothing but God! I am merely traveling the path set before me and putting complete faith in He who laid said path. At the end of the day, I just want to hear, "Well done!"

Have a blessed day on and in purpose!

CHAPTER 17

*I'm learning that it's in my best interest
to not have expectations of anyone.*

I've spent most of my life trying to make people happy with the expectation that it would be reciprocal. I've sat there and said things about what people have said or done because my expectation was that they should say or do things like I would say or do those things. I've expected people to treat me a certain way or match my effort because of the effort I was putting into them...all of which has lead me to this epiphany. "Expectation outside of necessity is a prelude to disappointment..."

I expect that I have to go to work if I want to get paid. I expect that if I go to work, I will get paid every two weeks. I expect that when I pay a bill, that I will get credit for the amount I paid. That's the way those things normally go, but even those aren't guaranteed. To go outside of those kinds of things and have the same level of expectations is just setting myself up. To expect people to act the way that I think they should is the very definition of insanity. The only expectation that I have of people nowadays is that they're going to be who they are regardless. Regardless of what I do to encourage, sway, or even mandate their behaviors regardless of how nice I am to them in hopes that they will do the same...regardless of how much they should do certain things because it's just the right thing to do. All of those things should matter, but the reality is that for the majority, it doesn't. Thus, two rules always apply...

1. Accept people where they are.
2. Deal with them accordingly.

I place my expectations of people within the confines of those two rules and when I do so, it clearly shows where the expectations should be placed... ME, MYSELF, and I... I can only expect that I am responsible for my actions and interactions when dealing with persons. I can only hold myself accountable for how I act and how I respond to actions taken against me. I can only place the expectation upon myself to hold what I say and do to a standard, regardless of whether it's reciprocated or not. I extend kindness whether it's given back or not...(like when I say hello to people as I pass them in the hallway and they say nothing in response or when I hold a door open for someone and they just walk in). I extend generosity regardless of how it's received... (I try to give something to those who are asking for help on street corners, whether it's the change in my pocket, most of the time, I give $1, or if I have food in my car that I'm not going to eat. What they do with it is on them). I extend an invitation of hospitality to those who may need it for whatever reason they may need it...(those who I hold close to me know I have an open door policy and me and my wife both honor it. If my friends and family need to come over for whatever reason and we're home, we're available...though many never utilize the resource).

At the end of the day, I will have to render an account for what I did, not what others did or did not do in response to it. I now focus on the expectations that I have in God's word and His promises and those expectations have yet to leave me disappointed. Those expectations have shown me that for a very long time, I've been putting my expectations in and on the wrong persons, places, and things. My God is the catalyst to everything and when I make Him the focus, the trickle down from my expectations connected to that focus is amazing. Today, I move forward knowing that man will never meet my expectations…they're not supposed to…that's a job tailor made for God…

Have a blessed day on and in purpose!

CHAPTER *18*

I apologize in advance for the long read.

God has powerful ways of reminding me that He's always there, even when I feel no one else is. This weekend, I was having a discussion about DJing. Someone knew someone who was interested in learning the craft and asked me if I gave classes. I explained that I do but I am selective of my pupils because it's an extreme investment of time and energy. I choose not to waste mine if the person is not genuinely interested in learning. I also stated that they need to know if their main reason to get into the art is to gain recognition, then this may not be the thing they want to get into because DJs are commonly the last to be recognized. At the end of parties, clients will acknowledge planners, committee members, caterers, facility owners, and even photographers, but rarely does the DJ end up on that list. So, if a person is not a space in their life being content with the fact that everyone had a good time being their recognition, then this art form may not be for them.

I learned that lesson a long time ago, but I get it… I'm human too. Who doesn't want "Good job" after a job well done? People really don't understand what goes into being a DJ and performing at an event. If a party is from 8:00 p.m. to 12:00 a.m., a DJ's hours are from 6:00 p.m. to 2:00 a.m., an average eight-hour day. A DJ has to load up equipment, get to the venue, set up said equipment, make sure everything is running properly, conduct sound checks for performers, and then perform at the event. After that, they load up the equipment again and then go home. During that time, a DJ deals with last minute changes and additions, answering questions for other components of the event that they're not responsible for, and requests! In the midst of things, making sure everyone enjoys their time. It's way more than what the average person sees when they attend events and rarely are DJs given credit for the work that they do.

Side note, I absolutely love the fact that my wife fully supports my passion and what I do. She is there at most events and she is my biggest fan and she's one of the main reasons that I can get up and do it weekend after weekend because I know she's got my back! He who found himself a wife has truly found a good thing! I have found an amazing blessing. This is just one of the many reasons I love me some Mrs. Wills!

I'm saying all this to say that this weekend, I provided sound for my church sponsored marriage retreat and needless to say that I worked all weekend between sessions and a party that took place on Saturday night. Other than the time we spent together at meals and at the party, my wife and I had very little time to ourselves. While couples were enjoying the getaway, I was setting up for the next event. Again, I love my wife for being understanding and supportive. Her energy helped me get through a very tiring weekend, which included losing an hour of much needed sleep. The conversation I spoke of initially was held on the Sunday at the last session we were having before being dismissed from a very empowering weekend of information, 657 revelations, and epiphanies. At the end of the session, they began to give thanks yous to those who helped put the event together. I had already postured myself to be left off the list as DJs most often are. But, not only did they announce my nam, but they announced and recognized my wife as well. Needless to say, I broke down. It was so overwhelming to me. I was then told afterward that they didn't want me to feel like they don't appreciate everything I do or feel that I'm being taken for granted. I knew that God heard my conversation and knew what I needed.

I had two takeaways from that experience. Firstly, I strive to remain humble because as an imperfect human, I take for granted daily what Jesus did for me when he sacrificed His perfect human life in order for me to be here today. I don't take into consideration everything involved in what He had to do to prepare for that moment, the behind the scenes of His ministry and the circumstances that leads Him to the cross to die for me. I thank everyone for everything *but* God! I go through life and forget to value what He did for me and the blessings He provides for me every day. I can look around me and see nothing but God and move forward without one thank you given to him, so who am I to complain when the same happens to me and I'm just me? That thought process keeps me grounded. Two… God knows what I need and when I need it and the closer I draw to Him, the more I see Him actively in my life. When He actively steps back to allow me to go through things so that when I come out on the other side of it, I see Him even more. He always has my back, He's always by my side, and He's always in front of me encouraging me to keep going to get to the end of my race so He can say, "Well done." It just makes me love my God even more.

It may seem like He's not there sometimes, but in all honestly I find that those were the times that I was looking to myself for the answers, not Him. I was relying on my own understanding, not His. I was too busy asking Him why instead of telling Him you are lord… "Your will be done." I received this weekend that faith the size of a mustard seed can move mountains. Because faith moves you stop looking straight ahead at the mountain, but rather look up to God which allows you to see over the mountain Food for thought.

Have a blessed day on and in purpose!

CHAPTER 19

Life experience is man's greatest teacher.
What we learn affects us far longer and
deeper than we will ever realize.

This weekend I watched the visions of others and a vision of my own come to fruition. I saw people come together collectively from different backgrounds, locations, lifestyles, and perspectives to achieve one goal—*greatness*! All were successful.

God has blessed me with a talent and with that talent, a purpose. He has surrounded me with person who are aware of that talent. What I am learning is that some people are in my space to help me in my journey as it relates to my talent. To assist, nurture, support, and push me to do what I am called to do. Some people are in my space because our talents and purposes compliment one another, one hand shakes the other, and that makes things mutually beneficial. Some people are in my space because my experiences when shared can help them in their journey and pursuit of their talents and purpose. It's important to know who is in my life and for what purpose. A lot of times, the reasons why I've found myself in complicated relationships, whether they be business or personal, is because I didn't take the time to assess where that person belongs in my life as it pertains to my purpose and calling. Our calling is not just for us to receive, but for us to give back as well. As we have been blessed, we must bless others. So that we may continue to be blessed...we cannot be selfish with what isn't even ours to begin with...but that's a story for a whole other conversation.

God leaves me with the responsibility of discerning what category people fall into in my life and governing myself accordingly. I consider it a blessing to have some who help me, some who I help, as we all help each other move forward. But I also have to be aware of who is in my immediate area and those who are trying to enter my space. The most important thing when it comes to living in purpose outside of a relationship with He who gave me my purpose is maintaining peace of mind and maintaining that peace of mind calls for the consistent and meticulous cleaning of house. Bottom line, I need to know who's in my house and why they're in my house, if they even need to be in my house to begin with, and if they don't then putting them out of my house.

I have never been so pumped about what my calling and purpose have in store for me because God is showing me why He gave me this gift. Now that I've surrendered to Him, He's showing me what He has in store for me and the beautiful people He's put in my life to help me get there. He has charged me with amazing people to help and support to get them to their calling and purpose. We get absolutely nowhere by ourselves because at the end of the day, we need God!

Have a blessed day on and in purpose!

CHAPTER 20

*What good is advice if you never listen to it
nor implement it in the process of making
the necessary changes in your life?*

When I look back at the some of the biggest mistakes I've made in life, I can also see that there were people in my life who advised me to handle things differently, and I didn't listen to them. When I attempted suicide, when I was hanging with the wrong people and my friends advised me what could happen and it did, when I refused to listen to my doctor, my first marriage, the list goes on and on. Pride comes before the fall. A lot of times, I refuse to listen to the advice of others because it conflicted with what I wanted to do. "No one is going to tell me what to do with my life. How dare they? Who do you think they are?" That's my pride talking. Pride is a very dangerous thing, which leads to much destruction when not balanced with logic, wisdom, and discernment. Pride is an emotion and we all know how making decisions while "In your feelings" works out… but I digress.

More importantly, God has been giving me advice my whole life that I've consistently ignored, and now I see what that life looks like void of Him. When I finally decided to surrender to Him, things became a lot clearer because I stopped trying to be God of my life and started to let go and let God be God of my life. I now see the persons, places, and things that He put in my life to assist me on this journey I now refer to as the beautiful struggle (Talib Kwali was a genius for that one!). Now I'm learning to listen when those who I know have my best interest at heart when they advise me on things. Pride is no longer a factor because I know my life, passion, calling, and purpose are not mine. I have been blessed to bring glory and honor to He who gave me those things. As a wise person once told me, "You hear everything, but you grow when you start listening, and you become wise when you begin applying what you heard." After all, wisdom is simply the application of knowledge... When you stop talking it and start walking it...

We have to start listening and not from a defensive place, but a place of understanding. We all can learn, we all can grow, and we all can become better than we were yesterday, but we have to be willing to listen and then apply sound advice when given.

Today I am thankful for all advice. I now know that the greatest advice comes a God who loves me unconditionally, and I am listening!

Have a blessed day on and in purpose!

CHAPTER *21*

*How can I be the best me I can be
if I don't know who me is?*

My thoughts this morning are in the hopes that someone who needs to hear this will receive what is said here. Diana Ross had a song, "Do You Know." I encourage you to take the time to read the lyrics, but the chorus goes:

> *Do you know*
> *Where you're going to?*
> *Do you like the things that life is showing you?*
> *Where are you going to?*
> *Do you know?*

You can have a car with a full tank of gas, money in your pocket, bags packed, and be ready to go, but if you don't have the destination, what are you doing? If you don't have an address to put in the GPS, how do you get there? Bottom line, how do you achieve your fullest potential and receive the blessings that are tailor made for you if you don't know who you are?

I went through the first part of my life trying to "find myself." It wasn't until I was separated and beginning the journey divorce and a few therapy sessions that I realized that I was rooming with myself but

I truly did not know who I was living with. I didn't know who I was because taking that look in the mirror was something I didn't have the courage to do. When I finally took that look, as much as I saw all my mess, I saw that it was my mess and my mess isn't half as bad as other people's mess. It's also mess that can be addressed, cleaned up, and removed. I also saw that I am blessed far beyond measure. Most importantly, I saw that God was there all along, waiting for me to see just how beautiful He made me in His image, imperfections and all. I learned to start loving myself...all of me. Not just the components of me that I thought others would like and appreciate, but all of me—the good, the bad, and the ugly. When I began to love and accept all of me, then what I needed in my life became clearer. Clearer still is what I *didn't* need in my life! Not too long after, one of the greatest blessings in my life came, and the rest is the present!

You have got to love you for you...all of you. Just like you have to get to know someone else in order to determine where that relationship will go, you have to learn who you are so that you then know how to love yourself because if you don't know how to...how will anyone else ever get it right? Better question, how will the right person get it right? How will you even know if they're the right person if you don't even know who you are? The change begins with you.

Our purpose...our calling...our journey...the path that is designed for us to travel is all based on the person God has designed us to be, and it's not until we discover, learn, take in, accept, embrace, love unconditionally, and enjoy that person wholeheartedly that we begin to see all the things that God truly has in store for us. Let today be the day that you begin to love God and let Him show you how to love yourself.

Have a blessed day on and in purpose!

CHAPTER 22

I don't know it all. I struggle, I cry, I question life, and I am still a standing member in the "Why me?" choir. I read 1 Corinthians 10:13 and go, "Yeah, right! People are always asking me questions or want advice. I'm looking at them like, "Who am I? I'm here trying to make a dollar out of fifteen cents, just like you." I'm a half step away from being on the news an hour early like any other person. I don't see myself as special in any capacity. I'm human like everyone else.

The past three years have been hell in a handcart, riding down a speed bump-infested road leading to a dismal abyss…paint a clear enough picture? But, it's when I paint that picture that I also see that I'm looking in the wrong direction. I'm looking down at the impending danger that awaits before me when I should be looking up to see that God is there with an extended hand, yearning for me to grab it so He can pull me out to safety. Never was I promised not to go through trials and tribulations. Never was it stated that my life would be roses and sunny days all the days of my life. I have lived life long enough to know that some days I'm going to wake up and not want to live this life anymore, but that's when I need to let go and let God. He's not going to beg me to let Him be who He is and has always been. He shouldn't have to…one of the greatest gifts He gave us, other than His Son, was the ability to delegate…

I am not the strong, wise man so many people think I am. This chest does *not* have an S on it. But I do know that my God provides and loves me in a big way and as long as I focus on Him…a way will be made…me still being here in spite of myself proves it. And for those who feel comfortable enough to share their life experiences with me and ask questions because they feel that I will give them an answer with their best interest at heart. The answer you get and that insight is not me. I am merely a vessel being used to shine His light into your life.

Have a blessed day on and in purpose!

CHAPTER 23

Just being real for a second, I shared this with one of my brothers and my wife this week, and I just feel that someone needs to here this… wrote a song about it…like to hear it??? Here it goes…

There will be times when I'm outside working on something or fixing something in the house and I'll come in the house and my wife will go… "Chris, you're bleeding!" I'll look down, and sure enough, there'd be blood. I didn't even realize it until she had something. I didn't feel it, so I had no way of knowing it was there nor the affects that it was having on me… I am coming to the realization that with the things that are going on in my life right now, God is trying to tell me something. Emotionally, mentally, and even spiritually, God is telling me… "Chris, you're bleeding!"… These experiences are showing me that life causes scars. In the process of trying to just get through it without showing up on the news an hour early, I have developed a tolerance for pain. For me, a high tolerance…to the point where I don't even realize that I'm bleeding. Can anyone relate? Just as when my wife tells me I'm bleeding and I go wash and tend to the wound, so to when I realize that I'm also bleeding emotionally, mentally, and spiritually. I need to go tend to those things as well. Otherwise, it can get infected. We know what can happen to an infection if not treated.

Some cuts are too deep to tend to on my own. Some need stitches, thus I have to get help from persons experienced in that area. There is absolutely nothing wrong with seeking professional help to assist you in your healing process. Not getting the help you need to heal is the equivalent of bleeding out, a slow and painful death. Who wants that? I know I don't. Do not be afraid to reach out for help! Look down, you're bleeding.

Have a blessed day on and in purpose!

CHAPTER 24

It's not that God isn't blessing you…you choose to
do nothing with the blessings you're being given.

A speaker was giving their presentation and while reading the tele-prompter, he stopped to explain that he was messing up some of the words because he misplaced his glasses. He stated that they were in the room somewhere and if anyone had seen them to let him know. A few seconds later, someone brought his glasses up to where they were during presenting. Thank yous were given and the presenter continued with the presentation and kept stumbling over the words. Never were the glasses used…

It's really easy for me to treat God this way.

1. I can go about life, business as usual, just because He gave me an answer. I can thank Him and resume my "I got this" mentality as if God didn't just bless me, like I did things on my own.
2. For whatever reason, I can take the blessing that God is giving me and sit it aside because I feel I don't need it right now so I'll save it for when I really need it. That way, I know it's already there when the time comes.

3. The blessing wasn't what I wanted it to be, what I expected it to look like, nor to the magnitude I feel it needed to be so I make the choice to not use it at all... SMH

The only thing worse than not receiving a blessing is receiving a blessing tailor made for you and allowing pride and imperfect human expectation to make you think the blessing is not good enough or that it should not be used.

If you are reading this, that means you woke up this morning...a blessing. You have the ability to read...another blessing! If you're reading this electronically, you have Internet access...another blessing! Please know that there are people who did not wake up this morning, lack the ability to read, or do not have Internet. Everything you do, can do, are trying to do, and will do are a direct result of blessings you've been given and taken advantage of. Don't act like you're the person responsible for the things you have. It is a dangerous mindset to have when *nothing* you have is yours!

I am nothing and I have nothing if I do not have God in my life, actively acknowledging Him in my life and striving to better my relationship with Him. Everything He provides me is a blessing that I intend to use to fullest, no matter how big or how small that blessing may be. Any blessing He gives is what I need at that time, and it's always right on time! Today I strive to use every blessing He has given me because life is not promised. Sometimes life is the biggest blessing we take for granted.

Have a blessed day on and in purpose!

CHAPTER 25

I remember my Dad and I working on a 1980 Ford Mustang. We took out the 4-cylinder engine and replaced it with an 8-cylinder 5.0 engine. He told me that we were working on it for a lady that he knew. She asked him to do the work. It never made sense to me. Why would a lady ask for an engine/transmission change like this? But if you know my Dad, you know he ain't not one question. I am an avid enjoyer of life and the pursuit of it…but I digress…

Weekend after weekend, while my friends were playing and hanging out, I was under this car, changing the transmission and taking out the engine piece by piece, bolt by bolt. To say it was a lot of work would be an understatement. There were times I wanted to skip steps, but I knew that it would affect the outcome of what we were working on. I wanted this lady, whoever she was, to be proud of the work we did. Finally, after long hard hours of blood, sweat, and tears…*literally*, we finished the project. She was running like a brand new car. Everything was working, no leaks or issues. I didn't want to see it go after all the time and energy we invested in it.

A week later, I went to take my driver's license test and passed on my first try. I was pumped! I had my license at 15 and 9 months, bragging that I got my license before I was 16. Didn't have care the first, but it didn't matter, I now had that plastic in my pocket. My mom already had my to-do list ready to go and I was for it. As we pulled up in front of the house, I saw a Ford Mustang parked across the street from our house. It was a different color, but I could recognize the car I'd been working on for months if I was blindfolded. I was in a state of confusement. Why was the lady here? What did we get wrong? What's not working? A myriad of questions flew through my head. I didn't see anyone in the car so I was even more confused. My mother and I got out the car. I kind of rushed to the house to meet this mystery lady whose request consumed months of my life, but when we walked in, it was just my dad sitting there watching TV.

"Is she here?" I asked

"Who, boy?" my dad replied

"The lady we worked on the car for. Isn't that her car out there?"

My mom interjected, "You mean *your* car?"

I turned around, and my mom was waving a set of keys. All that work, time, energy, commitment, blood, sweat, tears, frustration, and aggravation was all for me to be blessed in the end. It was a job well done and worth everything because of my own investment. I didn't even know it but I was being prepared for the blessing that was intended for me to receive.

The message? Know that *everything* you're going through has purpose. It's not always for you to know why. There's this thing called faith. What you need to know is that you're being forged for your blessing. Much like a caterpillar struggles and sometimes almost dies to get out of the cocoon so that it can emerge a beautiful butterfly, so too is the process of your emancipation into what God has had in store for you all along. Know that His plan is perfect; know that He does everything out of love; and know that if you didn't struggle, there's is absolutely *no way* you would fully appreciate what He has in store for you.

Have a blessed day on and in purpose!

CHAPTER 26

Today's thoughts are simple. I got a lot on my mind and as much as I want to share thoughts every day to encourage, inspire, and just help people see that they're not alone in their everyday struggle, some days, I struggle with my own existence. I am human just like everyone else. I have good days and I have bad days. I just have a perspective on life that helps me to put things where they need to be so that I can move forward. I have a faith that aids me in realizing that I cannot get through this life alone, nor void of His presence in it and the power He has over it. Knowing this keeps me anchored amidst the storms. There is something over the horizon because too much is happening right now, back to back to back and normally when that's the case, there's a plateau that the devil wishes me not to reach.

So, what I will say is stay strong…keep fighting…the finish line of this chapter of your life is in sight, don't stop running…dig down…dig deep. God is cheering you on. You can do it! You can do it! Know that you did not make it this far to be left here…and if you focus long enough, you will see that He's never left you.

Sorry y'all…that's all I got today…

Have a blessed day on and in purpose!

CHAPTER 27

My mother told me last night that experiences are like an anchor. They can either brace you to stand your ground amidst the storms or they can keep you stagnant and unable to move to the next level. It's all in how I choose to look at them. Even on the other side, she blesses me. I miss her so much.

My grandmother told me, "Never let what the devil says about your life distract you from what God is doing in your life." I miss her too. But then my other grandmother stood behind both of them and said, "God made your back too strong to not carry the weight He's put on it. But, boy, if you don't take care of your back, it will break. You can't be a Wills with a broken back."

It was so clear and vivid, an amazing picture of the women icons of my life. Now, normally, my mom visits me in my dreams. At first, it freaked me out because my sanity immediately came into question. Discussions with others who have lost parents helped me understand that it's not too far from the norm and some have advised me to listen intently when these dreams take place, and so I do…judge your grand sister, okay? LOL!

Every now and then, her mother, the first grandmother mentioned above, comes and imparts her wisdom as only she can. She was always a woman of few words, but those words would change your life if you listened closely. This was the first time my other grandmother came to me in a vision, on top of that joined the other female anchors of my life. It was amazing to see them together, which just amplified the wisdom they imparted upon me.

Sometimes we worry too much about where the knowledge is coming from instead of focusing on the knowledge and wisdom given. I don't care if people think I'm crazy. People will formulate their opinions after reading this, and that's fine. What I do know is what I was told I needed to hear. The confirmation of their happiness in heaven and the weight of their words uplifted me in ways words cannot fully convey.

I pray that you're impacted today by wise words from someone who holds you dear to their heart. Even better, I pray that you be the disseminator of those words to someone you know who is in need.

Mom and Grans…know that the tears I shed are tears of joy because your love has never left me and my love will never leave you all. Thank you so much for everything you all did while you were here and everything you're doing for me now from a much better place…much love and RIH!

Have a blessed day on and in purpose!

CHAPTER 28

There is something soothing about being near water, just sitting, doing nothing and listening as the water flows past. Whether on a stream or as rain flows down the street, the sound is therapeutic. I can't appreciate it fully if I'm moving around and doing other things. The sound of water is most effective when I am being still to appreciate all it's wondrous beauty. Peace, be still!

Sometimes, I have to stop. I have to take the time to digest, process, and prepare myself for the daily things I deal with and go through. The more I try to do right, the more the devil is going to throw everything, including the kitchen sink, at me. If I don't make the time to be still, reset, recharge, and regroup, then the next day I'd get weaker than the previous day. Eventually, I'm going to run out of gas and have nothing to offer myself or anyone else. I have to take time out for me. There's absolutely nothing wrong with that. I worry so much about letting people down that I neglect to take some time for me. That's exactly what I'm going to end up doing.

My mother always said, "By choice or by force." I knew exactly what she meant every time she said it with that look on her face as she stared at me over her glasses. With the hustle and bustle of my daily activities, the responsibilities of being a husband and a father, and struggling to maintain my spiritual walk in the process, I now see that I've had the order wrong all along. My focus on my spiritual walk will guide me in my responsibilities as a husband, a father, and a man in this way wicked world. I prefer to choose so that I no longer have to be forced to address the things that are there to simply help me be better.

Stop, take a deep breath, take another, and now take a minute to just reflect…just a minute. When that minute is over, realize that life hasn't passed you by. You didn't lose anything, your day will still continue, and your life will still go on after taking time out for yourself!

Have a blessed day on and in purpose!

CHAPTER 29

I am responsible for the words I choose to use to convey my thoughts. However, I am *not* responsible for other's interpretations of my words.

Way before Slick Rick and Biggie, Jesus was master of the art of storytelling. His parables are classics to this day and still paint clear pictures every time they're read. Part of my passion for analogies and picture painting stem from reading the visual wording of God's only begotten Son. There's something about when words make you envision clear thoughts of what's going on at the time. Anyone who loves to read novels can appreciate that concept. There's a skill set to that form of effective communication that is so dearly needed in our day and time, but I didress. There's something else that I've noticed about Jesus' words that spoke to me this morning. No matter how clear a picture his words painted or how vivid the message was conveyed, the people of that time still chose to interpret it to fit their needs and agendas and eventually used them to kill the Son of God.

That taught me a powerful message. The epiphany hit home again this morning. No matter how clear my verbiage or how finite my articulation of the message, those who are within earshot of those words will interpret it how they see fit. No matter what I say or how I say it, people will continue to hear what they want to hear. Based on where someone is in their walk in life, their experiences, knowledge base, wisdom quotient, etc., dictates how they receive a barrage of words coming in their direction. How close words come to hitting home affects a person's reception of the message. I'll just leave that there for now. Knowing this, it is my responsibility to be as clear and as vivid in my communication so that person who listens to the words will receive the message contained therein. The reality is that regardless of how articulate my word may be, there will still be those who contort, misinterpret, and just not understand the message for a plethora of reasons. I need to be okay with that because I did my part.

Jesus would deliver His message and keep it moving. If people had questions or needed further insight into the verbal pictures He painted, He never hesitated to stop and answer any and all questions. Some of the questions He answered He knew had ill intent or were an attempt to set Him up. He never let that stop Him from answering the questions and shedding more light on His message and gospel. Bottom line, Jesus made sure they got it even if they would never get it.

Today I accept that my responsibility is to communicate effectively the things I'm trying to get across or convey. What people choose to do with that information is entirely up to them. When I give money to a person holding a sign at a light, my responsibility ends at being a cheerful giver. I am not responsible for what that person chooses to do with the money I gave them. I now must adopt that mentality with the words I use and the conversations I have moving forward. I can only be responsible for my actions, both word and deed, and pray that those who will listen.

Be okay if the person who hears you isn't listening…you words are being spoken for and in purpose and although you plant seeds and water, know that only God can make it grow (1 Cor. 3:6–9).

Have a blessed day on and in purpose!

CHAPTER 30

It is absolutely ridiculous for me to think that over thirty years of bad habits are going to just go away simply because my convictions have changed. I struggle with the man I use to be versus the man I've chosen to become for every single day my eyes are allowed to open. Psychologically, my subconscious mind has accepted, confirmed, and substantiated that my current actions are simply the mandated way that I am to govern my life, make my decisions, and pattern my behaviors. I literally have to tell myself… I say self…self says huh?!?!? "Listen, self, today I will keep changing. I will keep moving forward. I will keep getting better." I have to change the thoughts in order for the actions to come to fruition.

It's a marathon process, not a sprint process. It takes consistent effort and reminders, and it's one of the hardest things I've ever invested time and energy in, but the outcome is so gratifying. Exercise is not just for the body, but also necessary for the mind and, more importantly, the spirit. My mantra is derived from Matthew 6:33 and 1 Corinthians 10:13.

Have a blessed day on and in purpose!

CHAPTER 31

*Therapy is a bad thing only if you
don't utilize the resource.*

When external scars heal, they may leave a mark as a reminder, but the process is completed. Mental and emotional scars are very different things. If not tended to properly, they never heal and spreads on to other things and experiences in our lives. There's no automatic or instinctual road map to mental and emotional healing. This is an area where we must look to GPS to be guided through. We must reach out to those with the expertise necessary to get us on the path to true healing and forward movement. Therapy is a blessing, not a curse. The misconception is that if you need therapy, you must be crazy. Well, guess what? We all are!

Now I say this with the understanding that God and His word comes first and foremost. He is the Alpha and Omega. In His infinite wisdom, He put persons, places, and things to help us in this journey called life. Therapists are one of those many resources. As of this writing, I am currently engaged in therapy. I discovered that I too need that GPS in my life because the roads I'm travelling in the process of healing have all turned out to be dead ends. I am getting the help I need to become a better me. It's the only way that I can help anyone else.

If you feel that things are becoming a bit much, that the weight you normally carry is getting more taxing than normal and you don't see a way out, first of all, seek your heavenly therapist and allow Him to provide the path to the earthly assistance that you need. We all need help. No one gets through any of this alone. The first step in getting help is admitting that you need it.

Have a blessed day on and in purpose!

CHAPTER 32

I do not serve a complicated God. Rather, I am a servant of God that chooses to make things complicated. He keeps things so simple and straightforward, yet at times I allow the machinations of His adversary to get me into so many things just to make it through the day. To a certain extent, that's very true. To navigate through this thing called life requires a plethora of things. Sometimes I depend strictly on myself. When I do that, it's easy to take things too far, read too far into what's necessary, and think too hard about the resolution to an issue I'm facing.

> *Me: I need to know the what, where, when, why, and how.*
> *God: Have faith in me (Jas. 2:14–26; Prov. 3:5–6; 2 Cor. 5:7).*
> *Me: My check was short. I got extra bills coming out this week. They're gonna take my house and my car. We won't be able to eat.*
> *God: Do not stress. Just seek my kingdom first. I got you (Matt. 6:25–34).*
> *Me: I'm scared. I know what I need to do, but I don't want to do it. I don't want to do it this way. When will I find that special someone? When will this or that happen in my life? I'm tired of things going the way they are going. I want this... I want that.*
> *God: Do as my son did (Lk. 22:42).*

Nothing good comes easy, and eoing what's right in a world that's lying in the power of the wicked most certainly isn't the easiest task. But serving the God who created the world that He's allowing His enemy to borrow, what do I have to fear? What do I have to worry? If I have faith that He is real and is active in my life, why do I continue to act like I'm on my own or it's me against the world? Faith the size of a mustard seed, do I really believe that?

Someone shared a quote with this week and it stuck with me. "There's no need to worry about tomorrow because God's already there." It's time that I start believing in that and not just saying it. It's time to let go and let God, no matter how fearful I get that I am no longer in control because the bottom line is I never was. It's time I stop working on 14/16 and break it down to 7/8, the LCD—a.k.a., the basics!

Life isn't complicated. *We are*! Better yet, we *choose* to be... Think I'm wrong? Try doing things His way, consistently, and let's circle back around and discuss that. Today I'm striving to keep my life simple by focusing on God.

Have a blessed day on and ins purpose!

CHAPTER 33

If I spend my life trying to please everyone,
I will die having never lived for myself
or, more importantly, for God!

I'm learning that as I live my life trying to please God, that path automatically reshapes my environment. It reorganizes the persons, places, and things that surround me on the daily. Since I wasn't seeing the people I used to hang around as much, I see with more clarity what God has put in my life. I even see what God put in my life that I may no longer need.

God made me who I am. As I accepted the path before me and the calling on my life, I realized that my sense of humor, my outlook on things, and my knowledge of movie quotes is not for everyone. They did not get it. Honestly, they're not meant to. It's not people I need to please, but God who has provided all.

To change who I am for the sake of people is to deny God and His purpose for my life. That's not an option for me. So those who come into my space have two options: to accept me for who I am, deal with me accordingly, and hopefully pray for my continued growth or to love me enough to leave me alone. I'm not here for y'all. I'm here for and because of Him!

Have a blessed day on and in purpose!

CHAPTER 34

I woke up today kind of meloncholy…
just bitter sweet.

I shed tears, but I'm ok. It's perfectly ok to miss my mother because she's not here and I'm okay with being sad. Something would be wrong with me if I wasn't. It's also the perfect time to reflect on what a blessing she was to me, the good times and the laughs we had, and the impact she had on my life. What an amazing, powerful, intelligent, loving, and faithful woman of God she was. I am proud to say that she was my mother. I share that sentiment with three generations of students, several generations of family and friends that still mention her to this day. She truly left her mark on this world…and on my heart.

On this day, I remember, reflect, recognize, and rejoice in the memories of a woman I know is looking down on me with that smile and her overwhelming love shines over my face like sunrise on a sandy shore.

I love you, Mom. I will never forget you. I will never forget what you did for me and the love you never hesitated to give to me. Rest in paradise! Top of Form

CHAPTER 35

I am my own worse judge. I rarely give myself credit, even for the things I've accomplished. I'm always striving to be better and do better. I don't acknowledge how far I've come in the process, just how far I need to go and how am I going to get there.

I'm learning that there is nothing wrong with acknowledging my accomplishments. There's nothing wrong with telling myself "Job well done!" The thing is, I need to do that more because when I do, I realize that I did nothing on my own. When I acknowledge what's been accomplished in my life, I admit that nothing is possible without God. So when I pat myself on the back, I immediately have to take that same hand and raise it high to give praise to Him who is truly worthy. My accomplishments becomes a constant reminder to me of who truly needs to be acknowledged. I am nothing without Him.

When I reflect, I can now see Him in everything. It's like a recap near the end of a mystery movie where they connect all the dots and you see the one person in all of the pictures they show. Then it all becomes clear to me who the real MVP is when I try to take credit for my life. It humbles me to be thankful for the life I've been given and the blessings bestowed upon me. I am in no way worthy of anything that I have, but that's the power of His love and grace. I have been blessed beyond measure. When I focus on my blessings versus what I feel I am lacking, my relationship with my Lord and Savior is strengthened and my love for him grows stronger. I have to develop a healthy balance of self-reflection and godly focus because it's the combination that leads to a life that is filled and happiness beyond measure. Today I strive to see God in me even more.

Have a blessed day on and in purpose!

CHAPTER 36

*You gotta get through because the blessing
is in how you got through it.*

The sun looks different to me after it's been raining for three days. That feeling the 1ˢᵗ day, I came outside and got in my car instead of walking to the bus stop because I didn't have my own transportation for a little over a year. I remember I had just moved into my apartment because I was beginning the journey of going through my separation/divorce and the peace and quiet that existed in those four walls was louder than anything I had ever heard before.

I am learning that the blessing *is* the lesson What I learn while I'm going through situations, trials, etc. increases my appreciation for everything after I've gotten through. The necessary change that has taken place is perception and direction. Where I look and how I look at things changes how I cope and deal with the circumstances placed before me. When it rains, I already know that the storm will *not* last forever so my attention is then directed to other things or other aspects of the storm. I'm now assessing the clouds, identifying patterns, and paying more attention to weather reports so I have more information ahead of time of future impending storms so I can prepare. The storms in my life are the *exact* same thing. They do not last for long. I've already been given the victory so now my attention goes toward other things. I'm now focused on what is to be taken from the experience, what lesson is there to be learned in what I'm going through, and how I prepare and fortify myself for the next set of circumstances that are sure to come from that have been promised to occur for the simple fact that I said Jesus is Lord. My focus is no longer now on God and His will for my life because He's already standing on the other side of every storm saying, "Come to me, and I will give you rest."

Nothing good comes easy. If it did, you would never appreciate it. Growing crops reaps the food to eat, but all the lessons and takeaways are in the process of growing the food. Nurturing the soil, plowing the fields, planting the seeds, and watering (the discipline, responsibility, accountability, and work builds character and ethics that can be applied to many other things. The blessing *is* the lesson and goes so much further than any food that comes from the experience.

At the end of the day, I'm not saying it's easy in any way, shape, or form. I can't stop the storms from coming. I have no power to deter what they bring with them. What I do have control over is how I go through them and the demeanor I possess as I get through and the praise and rejoicing I give after I've gotten through because I will get through! YOU WILL GET THROUGH!

Have a blessed day on and in purpose!

CHAPTER 37

None of us are immune from this thing called life. We all have to get through as best we can for as long as we're given breath each morning to live another day. No two snowflakes are the same, but at the end of the day, they're all snowflakes. I say that to say that we as human beings share more similarities than we realize. I am not the only one experiencing hardships and facing trials on a daily basis, but I can easily become consumed with just me. It takes nothing to lose sight of the world around me, the family and friends I hold dear, and even my own health. If I'm not careful, I can become the catalyst to the end of my existence instead the motivation of it's continuance.

For fear of being considered weak, inferior, less than, sub-par, etc…many hesitate to reach out and utilize resources that are right in front of us and easily accessible. Here's the hurtful truth and sad reality, if you're not striving to be better and do better, if you're not focusing on becoming the best man, woman, husband, wife, mother, father, or child of God, you are in fact already losing and far removed from the blessings being held out to you and for you.

We've got to do better, We've got to be better and it starts at home…its starts with taking that long, hard, and sobering look in the mirror and humbly opening our eyes. This is coming from a person who has done it and absolutely hated the shell of a man I saw struggling to look back at me. We all need help. None of us can do anything on our own. We are absolutely and unequivocally *nothing* without God.

I have begun the journey of therapy to aid me in becoming the best man I can be so that I can be a better child of God to my Father, the best husband to my wife, the best father to my children, and the best servant to those who I am called to serve. I am learning that everything I've been through was for me to get here and now a new chapter begins. Faith the size of a mustard seed is multifaceted and yet so simplistic at the same time.

I encourage anyone who reads this to seek out help or assistance. Bow down and pray that His will for your life be made abundantly clear because it is in that where all of the answers and your real blessings lie.

Have a blessed day on and in purpose!

CHAPTER 38

It's amazing the things that affect our current everyday behaviors that we never knew existed because we never took the time to see what we needed to heal from.

The human mind is an amazing thing and more powerful than most are willing to accept. One can literally achieve anything they seriously set their mind to. It's just that most do not strive to have the tools necessary to instruct the mind on how to do so.

I'm currently connecting the dots between what I do, how I live, and why I say and do the things I've been doing all along. If I want to become rich, then it's in my best interest to surround myself with those who are already where I want to be. The same goes for my mental wealth/health. We are programmed to believe that only crazy people see therapists…psychologists…etc., but to not seek help to better one's self…isn't that crazy? If I am not the best me, how can I truly be me best for anyone else, and more importantly, offer up first fruits to God? Today, I strive to keep moving forward as I acknowledge the things that got me where I am today. "Those who do not learn from their history are doomed to repeat it."

Have a blessed day on and in purpose!

CHAPTER 39

I am not perfect. I make mistakes. I fall flat on my face, get up, brush myself off, tell myself it's going to be okay, take two steps, and fall flat on my face again. I've repeated several grade levels in the School of Hard Knocks and sometimes failed the exact same class knowing it's the class I needed to pass in order to graduate. I will die striving for perfection knowing I will never attain it, but I *will* die striving. I will never claim to know it all, but I do know what I've learned thus far.

The past few years have taught me a lot. I learned that to repeat my mistakes is a choice. I have to choose to do better. In order to navigate through my present and into my future, I must take in a clear understanding of my past. I've learned that therapy is an absolute blessing. Only the powers that be who are under the influence of my God's adversary want me to believe otherwise because they know that mental, emotional, and spiritual clarity is a dangerous weapon. The greatest weapon the devil uses is ignorance. He prays—yes, the devil prays too—that we don't learn about ourselves, that we remain oblivious to how our bodies work, how our brain/mind functions. How great a genuinely intimate relationship with God can be. To coin his phrase that he used when speaking to Eve, for in that day he knows our eyes will be opened, and we will be like God, knowing good and bad. He knows that if we take the time to get to know ourselves by getting to know and coming to love God, that we will be unhooked from his Matrix. (I've said it before and I'll say it again, two of the most spiritual movies to date are "The Matrix" and "Inception"… but we can debate that later… I digress…)

It's not hard for me to change. I just didn't want to learn the process. I had grown comfortable in the life I'm living as I'm living it. It wasn't the best, but it was doable. It didn't cause any waves. It kept me under the radar. To change it may expose me for the sinner that I am. Then my God asked me, "Why are you hiding?"

I have been uncomfortable for some time now. From losing my mother, and both grandmothers in what felt like a Job effect to having my health attacked, almost not even being able to walk and potentially not being able to DJ anymore. To not knowing if I'm going to have a job every school year and even being threatened with a pay reduction. Consistent attacks on my marriage as I watch friends and family go through the same. Trying to maintain a relationship with my father when I've never had one to begin with and all the while keeping God as my focus because for most of my life, I've seen up close and personal who I am without Him. That discomfort has been the catalyst to some of the greatest revelations and epiphanies in my life. God placed some serious resources in my life that have given me hope and shown me that me staying off the radar is not for me to decide, in fact, none of it is… His will be done. I am not perfect. I make mistakes. I fall flat on my face, get up, brush myself off, tell myself it's going to be okay, take two steps and fall flat on my face again. But, now I focus on the blessing that God keeps helping me up…every time…

May you see that as imperfect as you may be, you are still amazingly and wonderfully made in His image. You just have to keep looking at Him and to Him to see that.

Have a blessed day on and in purpose!

CHAPTER 40

*I spend too much time being focused on
the wrong things for the wrong reasons.*

It is my natural inclination to want to do things my way, the way I see fit, the way that things work best for me. But it's not about me nor has it ever been. God, family, friends, and then maybe me. As I focus on the hierarchy of my life, I realize more and more that as my focus changes, my priorities and purpose become abundantly clear. The implementation of my calling becomes catalyst to a peace of mind I've never had before amidst the storm. It's not about me because it's no longer my will that needs to be done. As they said in *John Wick: Chapter 3—Parabellum*, "I have serve. I will be of service." Servants don't call the shots. They humbly submit and follow instructions with the hopes that who they serve has their best interest at heart. Hence… I serve a powerful and amazing God! Side note…even Jesus submitted himself and served the will of his Father. So who am I?

When I look at the things that went left in my life, I can clearly see that I and I alone made the decision to go in that direction. 9 times out of 10, doing so having the necessary information that that's not the best way to go or the best thing to do. Much like Frank Sinatra, I did it "my way" and dealt with the consequences of such a pride-filled approach. Not anymore. It matters not how others feel or even how I feel. My will is no longer the focus, but the will of He who purchased me with the blood of His Son. The risk is too great for me to do otherwise and has cost me too much as it is already. Today I reaffirm the choice I made to walk a path purposed for me and live up to the expectations of He who sacrificed so much for me, knowing I would never be worthy of the price He paid. His will and purpose becomes the priority. Anything else would be uncivilized.

Have a blessed day on and in purpose!

CHAPTER 41

My hypocrisy only goes so far.
                        —Doc Holiday.

Why is that I find myself more apt to listen to man than God? Case in point, if my car breaks down, I take it to a mechanic. If my computer acts up, I go to the Geek Squad. If my house needs repairs, I will call a contractor. But if my life ain't right, I won't call on God. I'll just figure it out on my own. I rely on my own understanding of something I know very little about. In all the other cases, when there's a problem, I go straight to the experts with no hesitation. I take their answer as scripture. The irony. I allow them to do whatever they deem is necessary to resolve the issue at hand. So, why do I fear He who I have faith in?

The fact is I don't fear Him, I fear having to look at myself. I don't like seeing close up how much of a wretch I am without Him and feeling like a failure because here I am again making mistakes and falling flat on my face again. It's not until I surrendered and gave Him the respect He's due that I realized that any character flaws He exposed was because they needed to be addressed, corrected, and or removed for my betterment. It's the same feeling when it was suggested I see a therapist. It wasn't that I didn't think they were qualified to help me. I just didn't feel that I needed help. I didn't want to face the feeling of being inferior by going for help and the lack of control I would have in the resolution. I'll let that sit for a minute.

I don't know everything, but one thing I do know is that if I can trust imperfect man with the things I need fixed. How much more should I be able to trust God with my life, especially when I already surrendered it to Him? My life is more important than any car, computer, house, etc. It's time for me to go to the expert and listen! Sometimes the answer we get isn't the answer we want, but that doesn't make it any less of an answer that we need or, for that matter, the right answer for us at that time. I didn't like half the answers my parents gave me. But being a parent myself, I get why they gave the answer they gave...leave even more reason for me to let go and let God.

Have a blessed day on and in purpose!

CHAPTER 42

I am still here to tell you about it.
I have had many experiences, good and bad.
I am still here to tell you about it.
I have been shot, survived several severe car accidents, and been in a major motorcycle accident.
I am still here to tell you about it.
I was diagnosed with a blood disorder and given three years to live.
I am still here to tell you about it.
I have a pinched nerve from two degenerative discs in my back that I will cope with for the rest of my life.
I am still here to tell you about it.
I was cut off by my parents for almost three years.
I am still here to tell you about it.
I was homeless for two years.
I am still here to tell you about it.
I was in a sheer hell of a marriage for seven years.
I am still here to tell you about it.
I lost my mother, her mother, and my father's mother in under a year.
I am still here to tell you about it.

I am constantly reminded of the mistakes I've
made and held to my past every day of my life.
I am still here to tell you about it.

On my worst day, God brought me through to see better days. As much as I can sit here and complain about the things I've been through and the hard life I've lived and am still living to a certain extent, the blessing is that I am still here, I am still alive, and I still have the ability to tell you about it. There are so many people who couldn't say the same. What I've just shared is a testimony of how blessed I am, not how troubled my life has been. It's when I began to look at it in that context that I can see clearly how powerful a God I serve and how true His words are in 1 Corinthians 10:13.

Know that you are here for a reason and a purpose because God makes no mistakes! Everything that has happened in your life has taken place with divine intent. It's only when you begin to serve your purpose that those intentions become clear. Then and only then!

Today, I am simply thankful, grateful, and overwhelmingly happy that I am still here to tell you about it!

Have a blessed day on and in purpose!

CHAPTER 43

There was a time when I quit DJing after my son was just born. I was told that I need to be a father and do what a father needs to do for his son. In my naivety, I listened. I sold my records (yeah… TIMESTAMP!), equipment, everything. Two legendary DJs in Baltimore sat me down and told me to think about what I was doing. They even joked that they would keep the records they purchased from me so when I came back, I could just buy them back from them. I made a pretty penny from what I sold so I got some things for my family. Then I got a part time job and worked on being a father.

Some time had passed, my brother got a residency at a local lounge. I would hang out with him from time to time. Every time I went, he would let me play a set. I was on cloud nine the whole time. Music was like a drug. I needed my fix for those few moments. This went on for a few months. One Saturday after I played my set at the end of the night, he sat me down and had a heart to heart with me.

> *Brother: This isn't just something you do in your spare time, this is something you were meant to do. I watch you when you're playing. This is your passion, dare I say, your calling. You have a God-given talent that shouldn't be thrown away.*
> *I: You may very well be right, but at this point, what can I do? I've sold all my stuff and invested the money in my family so unless a miracle happens, it is what it is."*

That was a Saturday night. That following Tuesday, I got a call.

Brother: What are you doing?
Me: I just got off work. What's up?
Him: Stop by my house. I need you to go somewhere with me.
Me: Okay.

We met up at his house hit the road in this van. While we're driving toward our destination, he told me that one of his friends just passed the bar and got a job with a big law firm. He was giving my brother all his equipment and records because he won't need them anymore. He wasn't even making my brother pay for any of it. We just needed to pick up the stuff. I thought, *It can't be much, but it's a start. I will be happy with whatever he has and maybe I can get back in the business again.* I was excited but refused to get my hopes up.

As we pulled up to the guy's house, he opened the door and greeted us. We both congratulated him on his current success. He led us to his basement. He opened the basement door and we went down a set of steps. When we got to the landing and turned the corner, I saw nothing but shelves of records. It took us two trips in my brother's van to haul all of them. I got back every record I sold and even got some that I didn't have because they were out of print. I will never forget as we were bringing the last crates (yes, crates) of records home, my brother said, "So what else does God have to do to show you that this is what He wants you to do?" I've been DJing for twenty years professionally as of July 2019.

When there is a calling on your life, there is nothing that can keep you from it and nothing God won't do to bring you to it. Never give up on your passion, your dreams, or your calling. They're tailor made for you.

Have a blessed day on and in purpose!

CHAPTER 44

What sacrifice is too great to make in your life?

I was in family group last night and had several epiphanies that have given me an even greater sense of urgency to get my life in order... (bare with me, this is a little long, but I promise I have a point to make).

If I were to offer you a valid winning Powerball ticket in the amount of 320 million dollars, but in order to get it, you had to sell all of your possessions, quit your job, and relocate. Would you be willing to make that sacrifice? If you're anything like me, half of that would be done before the terms and conditions were finished being communicated because I know I can replace those things with much better things. I may be sacrificing temporarily but the guaranteed replacement is worth far more. Now let that sit there... But what if the terms changed? What if you had to leave your family? What if you had to give up all hopes of having a family? What if you had to move to a foreign country and forbade contact with your family? What if you had to remain single for the rest of your life, does the offer still sound as good?

Last night, we read about the wealthy ruler who walked away mad because Jesus said in order to receive treasures in heaven, he had to give away all of his worldly possessions (Lk. 18:18–30). The epiphany was never about the ruler's wealth. It was about his heart and what he would be willing to do or sacrifice to be with God. Jesus guaranteed him treasures in heaven, but the man couldn't part with what he had to sacrifice to gain those treasures.

What am I not willing to sacrifice to be with God? Will I choose money, family, career, material possessions, or relationships over God? Am I not willing to sacrifice those things to attain treasures in heaven? What does my heart look like when it comes to my commitment to God?

While we were studying last night, I couldn't help but reflect on the faithful life my mother lived. Although I have many differences of opinion when it comes to the religion she chose, I cannot dispute that my mother left this earth a faithful lover of God. She was willing to sacrifice our relationship to assure her treasures in heaven. As much as it hurt then, I now model my life to mimic her faith. It's easy to make little sacrifices and say God is good, but when He does a heart check, will I walk away mad or say Jesus is Lord? If my heart is looking up toward God in all things, then the rest of me will follow suit to make sure I attain those treasures in heaven. My mother has been enjoying the fruits of heaven for three years now and is still teaching me lessons here on earth. *I love you, Mom!*

Bottom line, it's not about the job you have, the car you drive, the house you live in, and the money in your bank account. It's not about the family you have, the relationships you've been given, not even the children you've been given the biblical responsibility to raise. It's about your heart in all things.

Have a blessed day on and in purpose!

CHAPTER 45

Allow me to apologize in advance for this being all over the place.

In my experience, those who have an intimate relationship *with* God are less likely to ask *why* God. Many look at the water's surface unaware of the undertow until they step in and get swept away. Experience has made me look at life differently. My perspective before and after I got shot was different My insight before and after I lost my mother and grandmothers was different My motivation before and after my children were born was different My gratitude before and after I married my better half was different. If you live long enough, you learn things

That being said, what am I going to do with the things that I've learned? The answer to that question automatically dictates my actions thereafter. Once my dad taught me how to change a flat tire, I never had to call AAA when I was stuck on the side of the road. I did something with the things I learned. Once my brother taught me the fundamentals of DJing, I began molding my love of music into a passion that has been nothing but a blessing for me. I did something with the things I learned. Once I got my heart broken, I immediately changed my actions to ensure that would never happen again. I did something with the things I learned.

The one difference between knowledge and wisdom is *application*! A smart man knows, but a wise man does. I'll just let that sit there for a few. If I know better, I do better, right? So if I know God. nope, y'all ain't ready for that just yet. For me, it's time for my actions to mirror the knowledge I've gained to achieve the wisdom behind the knowledge I possess. No more running, no more hiding, and no resistance. Sometimes the only way a person can move forward is to first plant their feet. When you get that, nothing will stop you!

Have a blessed day on and in purpose!

CHAPTER 46

One of the hardest things in this life during
these dangerous times is to be a person that gets
it living in a world that is often clueless.

One aspect of that is trying to help people who say they want to be helped but only want you to help them their way on a way that's most comfortable and convenient for them. This can become very frustrating and, quite honestly, extremely draining when people are constantly asking for your help but then get upset with you because your "help" makes them accountable and responsible for their own actions. I never wanted to be the person people come to. I just want to live my life in peace and quiet and work on becoming the best person I can be for me and my family. That's not the case. My wife will tell you that I am the first person people call when things go down. People reach out to me before they reach out to the people closest to them. They want my viewpoint on everything. I constantly ask what makes my outlook on things so important to others. It can be overwhelming at times.

We all have a calling, a purpose that we've been put on the earth to serve and accomplish. With that purpose comes a molding and building process that take us outside of our comfort zone majority of the time. When we ignore or fight against that calling and or purpose, it just makes the whole process even more difficult. "By choice

93

or by force are the only two options we have," my mother used to always say and to try to run away from what we are destined to do is equivalent to running away from a horror movie killer on a treadmill. So if my purpose is to support, encourage, and a relay the cold hard facts of this world we live in and how it works, then so be it. I will no longer be is a person who runs from the very calling that I've been given.

Nothing in this world comes easy. We are going to acquire scrapes, bumps, and bruises along the way, but the worse things is for those scars to be self-inflicted because we refuse to do things any other way but our way. Our life isn't even ours to begin with, but it's a blessing we are graciously extended every day. Our way is futile because we are a mess, point, blank, period.

So, if my purpose is to be support, encouragement, and a relayer of the cold hard facts of this world we live in and how it works, then so be it. But, what I will no longer be is a person who runs from the very calling that I've been given.

I hope y'all are ready because it's about to get real!

Have a blessed day on and in purpose!

CHAPTER 47

As I am learning more about the calling on my life and the purpose I am being held accountable to serve, I am learning that it is not my responsibility to please people. Now let me be clear, there is a vast difference between wanting people to be happy, specifically those I hold dear, and spending my time attempting to be the catalyst to said happiness. Basically, it is not my job to live my life to bring you happiness. It is my calling to strive to live my best life in the will that has been placed upon it…and through me living in my purpose shines light on how good God is in hopes that others will want to find out for themselves how good God can be in theirs.

John 3:17, the Message Bible Version says God didn't go to all the trouble of sending his Son merely to point an accusing finger, telling the world how bad it was. He came to help, to put the world right again. I am not here to point fingers. I am not here to tickle the ears of those who merely want to hear what they want to hear to justify the path they've chosen to walk, just like the wealthy ruler who approached Jesus. I am not here to judge, I am here to tell the truth. What people choose to do with it is not on me, but know that once information has been given, we are then responsible for what we do with it.

I can't live anyone else's life. To be honest, I don't want to or care to. I love my life and everything that comes with it…the good, the bad, and the ugly. What I can do is share my life in hopes that it will encourage, uplift, shed light, and even warn people against paths they need not tread. I can share in hopes that person will realize that none of us are alone in this thing called life. We're all in it together whether we like it or not. Sometimes just knowing that can be the beginning of something great! Today I accept that I am not living my life for you, I'm living my life for me. More importantly, I'm living my life for God.

Have a blessed day on and in purpose!

CHAPTER 48

I may not agree with what someone chooses to eat, but at the end of the day, what they eat will never make me go to the bathroom.

We all have choices to make. We all make good ones and bad ones. I recognize that it's our own individual choice to make, not anyone else's. If I care about you, I will always share my knowledge and sometimes wisdom in hopes that someone will not have to walk down the painful roads I've traveled. At no time do I have the expectation that just because I said something to someone that they will immediately turn around and change their life. I don't tell anyone anything with the goal to persuade them. I share information so that when the time comes for that information to be utilized, they will *not* be able to say that I didn't share it with them. It becomes their responsibility. What that person does with the information is up to them. Bottom line, once information is disseminated, a person can no longer say in in good conscience, "I didn't know." Even in law, ignorance is no excuse, but I digress.

The lesson I'm learning is that my job is to plant and water became only God can make it grow (1 Cor. 3:6–9). I can encourage, offer advice, and share information, but I have to accept that what a person chooses to do with any or all of that is entirely up to them. I need to be okay with whatever they decide. That's the hard part because when you care about people, you always want what's best for them. But I'm learning that they have to want what's best for them first. Bottom line, the only life I can actively change is my own. and that's the journey I continue today.

We all have choices to make, but more importantly we all have to accept the choices being made, even if no choice is being made at all.

Have a blessed day on and in purpose!

CHAPTER 49

*Sometimes the best way to love someone is from a
distance because I need to love myself up close.*

It's hard to get people to understand that I didn't stop caring about
them. I just learned the lesson they were placed in my space to teach
me. When I graduated from 1st grade, I didn't leave the school, but I
didn't need to sit in that classroom anymore because the knowledge I
needed to acquire had been attained. I may walk past the class from
time to time and chat it up with my old teacher, but then I go to the
class I am now enrolled in and strive to keep moving forward in my
academic career.

There are times in my life where the lessons come from people
instead of classrooms, but the purpose is the same, my growth and
development. Just like it would never make sense for a person who
graduated from 1st grade to voluntarily remain in that same class for
years afterward. It makes no sense to stay in the same space or around
the same people after they have served their purpose. To some that
may sound a bit on the brisk side, but staying in unhealthy relationships that have run their course or relationships that should have
never been relationships in the first place can never be a good thing.
Doing things just to satisfy others at the expense of myself is one of
the *worst* decisions I can make in my life! A reason, a season, or a
lifetime—it takes discernment to make the proper determination of

who gets which title. It takes knowledge of God and self to achieve true discernment. But I digress.

I have to be okay with letting some people go because it was never their purpose to stay (let that marinate…). But, I also have to know myself and more importantly, I have to love myself in order to truly be okay with the decisions that I have to make that will prove best for my life and the purpose I am meant to serve. My life is bigger than me. Today I am learning that it's not always a sacrifice, but implementation of lessons effectively learned.

Have a blessed day on and in purpose!

CHAPTER 50

*Now I see why He never wanted us to partake
of the fruit. He made us in His image but
never intended for us to be like Him.*

I am far from perfect but at the end of the day, I'm not a bad dude. I feel I bring a lot of things to the table, and to God I will always give the glory for that I because it's definitely not me alone being the best me I can be, I am nothing without Him. With all the knowledge I've acquired, wisdom I've gain, and life experience I've incurred, I do *not* want my children to be me nor be like me. I want them to be the best them they can be. Ultimately, I want them to be better than me. I don't want them to make the mistakes I've made or experience the hurts I've endured. I want them to take what I've passed down to them and forge their own path. Although they come from us, our children should not become us. We offer all we have to them in hopes that they will utilize it to become their own best self, not another version of their ancestry.

God gave Adam a planet full of creation. He gave him ownership over it and responsibility over naming the creatures, plant life, and everything in it. He provided an environment in which he could become his own best self. He was even provided a helpmeet taken from his own rib who would become his better half. Somewhere along the journey of bettering themselves, they became focused on becoming better than themselves. You missed that one right there, but it's okay. Moral of the story, for Adam, Eve, and Satan... In an attempt to be like God, all they did was remove themselves further from Him and the purpose He had for them because it was never meant for them to be anyone else other than themselves. Adam and Eve lost perfection in an attempt to gain something that was never theirs to have. The devil was cast down to earth permanently and is now roaming it like a lion seeking someone to devour because he desired a throne that was never meant for him to be seated upon.

When I yearn for and pursue the things that belong to and are meant for someone else, I am plotting my own self destruction. Much like He did Adam, God provided me with so many resources. He's also given me responsibilities and tasks to accomplish, He's given me a purpose that only I can fulfill to the extent He wishes it done. It's only when I focus on myself or desire something that that belongs to someone else that I lose sight of my purpose and the grand blessings that God has in store for me in my life. Today I am learning to continue striving to be the best me because that's what God has willed for my life. God doesn't want me to be Him because He knows that I would never be able to handle that even if He gave it to me (Don't let *Bruce Almighty* fool you!). He merely wants me to be the best me I can be because I would become a shining reflection of Him.

Have a blessed day on and in purpose!

CHAPTER 51

It's okay to be me even if no one gets me because at the end of the day, God got me.

I've always been on the outside looking in. All of my childhood, teenage years, and the majority of my adulthood, I've been in the space of the cool or popular folks, but I've never truly been one myself. Even when I modeled clothes, I was only in the public eye on stage. As soon as the show was over, it was back to the normal regiment of being walked past in the crowd. Sounds quite sucky, huh? Well, not for me. Being on the outside and not being the focal point allowed me the opportunity to observe people and their behaviors in their natural environments, unaware of my existence. I was able to see how people really conduct themselves, see their true character, and assess what makes people do the things they do. I would go to the library and read up on basic psychology to connect the dots of what I saw. Even now, figuring a person out quickly still remains one of my fundamental defense mechanisms. The quicker I can determine who they are, the quicker I can assess how close you need to be to me to serve your purpose, if you even need to be there at all.

So my being a loner and outcast helped mold me into the person I am today and hone my abilities to look past a person's surface and see someone for who they really are. But I digress. Being able to see a person's personality trait changes your entire perception of them and everything they say and do, not from a negative perspective but a deeper insight. Discovering a person's motivations is a very powerful gift to have. Along with a high emotional IQ, as my therapist pointed out, I can see things way differently than most. Like the way Neo saw things at the end of *The Matrix*. The thing is, when you see things differently, it means that most may not be able to comprehend what you see. I'm learning that that's okay! Not everyone is meant to see your vision. Not everyone will acknowledge or appreciate your talents, your gifts, your insight, your knowledge, your wisdom, etc. not everyone will see your path for the beautiful journey that it is. That's okay. As long as you do!

You are wonderfully made. Every single thing you've gone through, every single segment of your life that you've experienced, no matter how great or how gruesome, was on and in purpose for you to learn a lesson that would mold you into the person God is calling you to be. Know that half of things you've gone through in your life weren't even for you, but so that you could be a blessing to someone else but that's a thought for another day.

I am learning that even though my thoughts and perception may be unique, I am never alone. First and foremost, my God is with me and has been with me every step of the way, even when I didn't believe He was real. Second, He provides the necessary resources to aid me on my journey. I've been blessed to be able to identify who most of those persons, places, and things are. I am truly thankful and grateful. Today, I am okay being me. If no one gets me or my thoughts, if no one can grasp why I'm doing what I'm doing, and if people look at me like I'm crazy, I will be absolutely fine with it because I know one person who gets it and what he's going to give me for it, no one else can provide.

Have a blessed day on and in purpose!

CHAPTER 52

Soft people have a difficult time
accepting the hard truth.

In a world of *Fifty Shades of Grey*, people are no longer able to easily digest things that are black and white. The issue becomes, does that make the truth any less valid? Does the concept of right or wrong become so diluted that it should cease to exist?

These are my thoughts this morning because I find myself in a bit of a quandary. The conversation I find myself involved in have very black and white implication, but people choose to stay in the gray because it's more comfortable. There is no accountability or responsibility to be found in that hue. Sooner or later, a stand must be made.

There is no easy way to tell someone that their breath is a little "tart," but when they're spewing out a bunch of strong h words in the near vicinity of your nasal passages, something must be said. If someone is having a heart to heart with you up close and personal and their breath is smelling like skin on a hot muffler and regret, you're telling me so as not to offend, you would remain tortured in silence? How does one know that there is an issue that needs to be addressed if it's never mentioned? How can one come to any resolve when they are left under the impression that a problem doesn't exist at all? Nothing good comes easy and change is never a smoothly paved road to travel, but we must travel down it nonetheless. The moment we're no longer afraid to speak the truth is the moment we will begin to see change.

Today I am learning that I can never be wrong for speaking the truth. It is my responsibility to articulate responsibly with the feelings of those involved in mind, but at the end of the day, the truth must be told. Grey is no longer a good color for me. Black and white has always been more functional for me any way.

Have a blessed day on and in purpose!

CHAPTER 53

When you point a finger at someone, there are
always three fingers pointing back at you.

Self-righteousness is such an easy and seemingly harmless attribute to convey, but it also affects my heart when it comes to my willingness to serve. If it is in my ability to do so, I am always willing to serve. When DJs hit me up for music, advice, or even want to take some classes, all I say is, "Let me know when and we'll set something up." My wife will tell you our home has an open door policy to many. I'm thankful that her heart is just like mine when it comes to helping others. The same courtesy extended to family, friends, and anyone who I can serve and help because I am *slowly* accepting what I'm called to do. But when I need help or support, it's not as easily found.

Now don't get me wrong, I know that there are certain people I can call on who will drop what they're doing to help me. I'm thankful that they have a heart to serve and share. There are instances when I need help and they cannot necessarily assist. Others should be more than willing to help, but they don't. I may be short a couple of dollars, but no one can spot me until I get paid. I may need to bend someone's ear just to get something off my chest, but they never respond back. I may need help setting up equipment at church, but no one shows up. All legitimate circumstances. I'm inclined to believe that it's not just me that experiences this.

Now the self-righteous me will kick in almost immediately. I've loaned people my last dollar but I can't get a few dollars to get me through? I always pay people back, I'm good for it. So what's the issue? My phone is always ringing, all day and night. I never turn anyone away. I've lost sleep at times when I'm exhausted, but I know how important some conversations are and the importance of having someone to confide in. I DJ all weekend, setting up equipment and performing. I have a pinched nerve and bad back. I get home at 3:00 a.m. and got right back up to set up for church. No one can wake up early to help for church?

Did you see how many *Is* were in that last paragraph? I lost count, and I wrote it…lol… As legitimate as each statement was, they were void of one thing…grace. As much as I go through things, so does everyone else, and to hold people at a level of expectation based on what I would do and how I would do it is a very dangerous space to be in because what if Jesus held me to the same level of expectation? What if my salvation depended on living my life as He did on earth, perfect and blameless? I was immediately humbled the instant I look at it in the right perspective. As valid as each statement was, I have to reflect on my heart when I make them. Am I focused on my service and my calling? See, when I have to render my account, it won't matter what anyone else did or did not do. It won't matter what they did to me or what they refused to do for me. At that time, I will be responsible for what I choose to do in my life specifically in those situations and circumstances. So what matters in that even if no one else gives to me, that I keep on giving. Even if no one else listens to me, I keep on listening. If no one ever serves me, I continue to serve. It matters what I do in all situations and circumstances.

Today I am striving to keep my heart in the right place and focus, to remain determined, and to continue doing what I am called to do, regardless of if it's done for me. My purpose is to serve. I must continue to move on with purpose.

Have a blessed day on and in purpose!

CHAPTER 54

I know most won't read this one, but it's on my spirit to share, and if a man can build an ark at a time when it has never rained, I can write these words. So here it is.

There is nothing I won't do for my family. I do all I can to provide for them and make sure they have what they need. I don't have a lot, but what I do have is theirs without question. I am struggling with the word *failure* because I always see others doing so much more. It's human nature for me to feel less because I can't do that. I constantly struggle because of bad decisions I made in my past that haunt my future decisions for my family. I'm in the process of cleaning up four decades of not caring for what I did financially. Not being able to make moves right now constantly weighs heavy on my heart. I have an amazing wife and two beautiful kids. I want to give them the world for them to want for nothing. God willing, I'm on my way to doing that. God is blessing me in ways I never thought possible. It's a humbling experience to see what God can do when you fully and intentionally acknowledge Him and allow Jesus to become Lord of your life. But I digress.

This is why I'm saying all this.

If I do put myself in a position to provide financially for my family. Even if that's all I do, I have still failed my family tremendously. What good is a trust fund if when they leave this earth and there has been no investment made in their spiritual wealth? If I leave them millions of dollars in a life insurance policy but I haven't shown them that the greater reward is to store their treasures in heaven, have I really created a legacy that they will benefit from? Matthew 6:19–21 is very profound and reminds me where my focus needs to be. Don't get me wrong, we need money to survive and make it from day to day, but my relationship with God has led to all my provisions being taken care of and more time for me to be with my family. That's the missing component I see when I look around. I'm not rich. I'm not making six figures, but me and my family's *needs* are always met. It's a testimony to Matthew 6:33.

In the quest for earthly riches, many have sacrificed their soul. The only way I can survive and succeed is by me putting my faith in He who has paved the way for my success. It's my relationship with Him that makes the path clear and the journey full of purpose. That's where true wealth is. No amount of money can equate that. I know many will disagree with that statement, but the peace of mind I am acquiring with each passing day tells me otherwise.

So today I am learning that I am richer than most. My investments are sound because they're not put in the temporary things of this world. My investments are where I want me and my family to go. My friendly reminder is that it's better for me to do everything in my power to get me and my family to heaven only to discover that heaven doesn't exist than for me to do nothing to get me and my family to heaven only to discover that it does.

Have a blessed day on and in purpose!

CHAPTER 55

I've set myself up for disappointment the moment I start expecting people to do or say things the way I do. Who am I to have that expectation of others?

Self-righteousness makes sense depending on which side of a situation you're on. Lately I have been asking for help setting up equipment. With degenerative arthritis and a pinched nerve, I have good days and bad days. I was simply asking for assistance so that the pain I endure every day would not escalate. Every week, I found myself by myself setting up equipment. If I can get up early in the morning after working late the night before and set up equipment with my bad back, why is it so hard for someone else to do this or at least help? Why is it that I've asked time and time again and no one is willing to help, but I drop what I'm doing and go help others when they need me? If I can do this, why can't they? Bottom line, when I stand before my God and face judgment, it will be about all of the things I did, the things I said, and the life I lived. At no time will what anyone else play a factor in His decision. What someone else did or did not do is irrelevant when it comes to how I choose to govern myself, my actions, my words, etc. I am responsible for how I choose to live my life, not for how I feel others should live theirs.

Now this doesn't mean I stop caring, stop giving, stop sacrificing, or any of that I am responsible for what I do. Galatians 6:1–10 is a powerful scripture for me because it teaches me to focus on my own accountability in serving and helping others. That even as I struggle with getting my own imperfect and wretched life together that it may still be necessary for me to carry the burdens of those who are not as strong as me until they get to point where they can carry their own burden on their own. Bottom line, I cannot get through this life by myself, but I definitely will not get through this life thinking everyone should be like me. Rather, I should do my part so that everyone would strive to be more like God, including myself. When my thoughts start to drift toward "If I can do it, why can't they?", then my thoughts are now focused on me and not God. Self-righteousness is a dangerous and toxic sin than can easily go overlooked.

Today my focus is to strive to live a life that my God will be pleased. My prayer is that others will do the same.

Have a blessed day on and in purpose!

CHAPTER 56

And if you could see inside my heart
You would see loneliness
And if I could show you my mind
You would be depressed

So I sit away lonely
And I get away only in my mind
Said, I sit away lonely
And I get away sometimes

This is one of my favorite Boyz II Men songs. I know it may seem like a redundant theme, but people really don't know or care about what I go through. I'm not talking about family, friends, and loved ones who are constantly there for me and I for them. I'm talking about once I leave my house and venture out into the world, no one could care less. Everyone is out for themselves, and the persons with a selfless mentality or a "communal" frame of mind make up a small minority. So what does that leave me with? A bunch of people at work, trying to conduct business, whose only focus is satisfying their selfish desires and wants. How does a sane person...well, somewhat sane, function in insanity? Just ask Jesus.

I'm only human. If you cut me, I do bleed. It's hard to be an empath in today's society. It's difficult to be a person who genuinely wants to help in a world that only cares about what they can take. It's a struggle just to be nice to someone for fear of how they will react. Doesn't that sound crazy? Everything I was raised to be now makes me a "soft" target, and my skin color does *not* help. How am I supposed to function in that reality day in and day out? This society is not made for the weak. It is designed to make a person weak, thus they can control the weak-minded, the weak-hearted, and the weak-spirited. The Willie Lynch letters still holds true with one purpose in mind, and they've been utilizing its premise for centuries. Keep the body but destroy the mind.

There's only one thing that helps me to keep it together. At the end of the day, one fact remains and that's where my sanity lies. As much as I love my wife and truly value her presence in my life; as much as my children motivate me to strive to be the best example I can be, to be better, do better, and keep moving forward; as much as I cherish my quiet time, sitting at my mother's gravesite and catching her up everything, knowing she's watching my every move; and even my time with my brothers and sisters I share my life with so that I can be held accountable for what I do in life as it pertains to my relationship with Christ, the one thing that holds me together and glues the shattered fragment of my existent into a resemblance of who I am today is God! I enter into a world completely controlled by His adversary. Every single day that I am allowed to live. How else do I possibly survive it? Satan has his own team. I'm not going to make it leaning on my own understanding. The primary enemy of God has been around for thousands of years, perfecting his craft. Having never played chess, I'm not going to sit down in front of a veteran and win. I can't step into the ring with Mayweather, having never boxed a day in my life, and think I'm going to knock him out. I'm not going to step on the court with Lebron and shut him down? None of that makes sense, but that's how I lived my life with my salvation at stake. Not anymore. Show me a person who can name one thing more important than my salvation, and I'll show you a person whose perception needs serious adjustment.

I struggle with falling off the edge every day. If I were to show you my mind and what I process, evaluate, struggle with, fight over, fight for, fight against, you would wonder how I smile, laugh, joke, go through life with joy in my heart. Like I said, that Boyz II Men song is one of my favorites, the difference being is now I know that after I sit away, I stand up and start walking again, knowing whose loving arms I'm in and who has my back. I now know that this is all the devil's way of keeping the pressure on because he knows if I get this thing on right, I'm going to be a problem. Well, no disrespect, but too late!

It's okay to be human. It's okay to have morals, values, principles, standards, and requirements. It's okay to hold accountable and be held accountable. It's okay to do the right thing because that's what we're called to do, who we're called to be. The struggle will come with living regardless, so today I am determined that if I'm going to struggle, then I'm going to do so with the best outcome for myself in mind. I going to live my life with purpose. To God be the glory!

Have a blessed day on and in purpose!

CHAPTER 57

*I will die imperfect, but I will
die striving for perfection.*

I am human. I make mistakes. I fall down. My decisions aren't always the best. I struggle, I cry, I have fears, I hurt, and I get depressed. I miss my mother when life becomes a bit much. I don't particularly care for my job. I find myself wanting to cause physical harm to persons for a plethora of reasons. I don't like what our society has become and how toxic the people are in it. I deal with *all* of these things and fight other demons on a daily basis, but most will never know what goes on behind these glasses and smile (But feel free to ask, and I will share because I am learning that there is a freedom in transparency that many just don't get.). These things do *not* define who I am. They are merely elements used to forge me into the man I choose to be and am being called to become.

Perspective changes intentions and actions. If I focus on the negatives on any situation, my actions and the outcome reflect that. So if I focus on the positives, there is nothing I can't accomplish. I know that is easier said than done, but the words still hold true nonetheless. Funny thing, my work mother, God rest her soul, would come to me almost every day and propose a scenario and challenge me to state the positive despite the situation or set of circumstances. It became frustrating to her because no matter what she came up with, I could find the silver lining to every cloud. I realize that I've gotten away from that. There are too many blessings in life to spend it focused on the things that deter me from acknowledging the blessings right in front of me. First Corinthians 10:13 tells me that the only reason I will fail and remain a failure is if I choose to think about that for a second. Yes, I will fail at times, that comes with life, but it never meant for me to stay there. If I do, it's because I have chosen to remain in that space.

We have a tendency to give too many external factors power over our internal peace. That just adds up to defeat. Outside validation is the deadliest drug in existence. The problem is, many don't even realize or want to admit that they're addicted.

I'm learning in church that knowledge of self is the most powerful tool in moving forward. I have to assess where I'm at in order to determine what direction I need to move and intentionally strategize how to get there. Many are lost and continue to ask other lost persons around them for directions. Even worse, they are too prideful to ask for directions at all. Today, I'm learning even more who I am, who I am being called to be, the direction my life needs to go, and how I am supposed to get there. At the end of the day, I am human. That's why I will never forget that that's the exact reason why I need God.

Have a blessed day on and in purpose!

CHAPTER 58

It's not you. it's me. Even when
it is you, It's still me.

With each passing day, I am learning that as I point one finger at people, places, and things, there are still three fingers pointing back at me. For so long, I expected the things around me to change. That the adaptation should be done externally for my benefit.

Hear how that sounds?

No matter what the situation is, no matter what set of circumstances I am facing, and no matter how much I am right about whatever is taking place, the change begins with me! I've spoken before about being fearful of becoming self-righteous and the sin that exists in that mentality, but here's something else I am now considering. If my focus is on what needs to happen in my life, the changes that I need to work on to become a better me and more importantly, a better vessel to be used in God's service. My personal relationship with Him and my progress in my spiritual maturity. If I am truly focused on getting my life right, I don't have time to worry about what other people are or are not doing. If I'm always worried about others, then that means I am neglecting myself in some way shape or form, which is probably why I'm too busy trying to check them when I should be checking myself. Let that marinate for a few.

Now I am not saying that we shouldn't care about others. Love is the identifying mark of any true Christian. It separates the wheat from the weeds, but I digress. I will always care about my fellow man. I will always want to see others succeed and be at their best. I will always want what's best for a person, regardless of whether they have the ability at that time to see it or not. But I can no longer expect someone else to think, feel, act, or in any way be like me. Matter of fact, at this point in my life, I wouldn't wish that on my worst enemy anyway, but the reason why is a story for another time.

The air mask on the plane remains a life lesson for me. I have got to put mine on first before I try to assist someone in putting theirs on. I've got to get me straight before I can truly be of any assistance to anyone else, which means I don't have time to worry about you or spend energy somewhere where it need not be. Today I am learning that when I look at something or someone, it's automatic to look at my heart to see if it's where it needs to be because when the heart's not right…well.

Have a blessed day on and in purpose!

CHAPTER *59*

*The epiphany is just crossing the
starting line in a marathon.*

Acknowledgment and acceptance is the catalyst to growth and maturity. But a catalyst is nothing if not followed with implementation and consistent work. To me, a catalyst is nothing more than a New Year's resolution if all I do is say what I'm going to do and say what I'm going to do and state what I'm going to change but do not implement a plan and stick to it. Well, I realized that as much as I am a work in progress, that means absolutely nothing if I'm not working *on* my progress!

Admitting I have a problem is the first step among many. For far too long, I've left it at acknowledgment as if that was enough. That's why I love epiphanies, even if it makes me aware of something I'm lacking in and need to work on. The fact that it's now clear to me is an amazing thing, and I am thankful and humbled in being shown, but I must act on what I now know if I am truly going to gain the wisdom I need to get through this thing called life.

As I stated in the beginning, this is a marathon. To run a marathon, it takes, practice, training, and a game plan. I will not just wake up one morning and years of mistakes, wrong thinking, and sinful behavior are gone. *Poof!* Still I am determined to keep working on the changes necessary to help me do better and be better. Today is the beginning of my revised game plan to become a better me.

Have a blessed day on and in purpose!

CHAPTER 60

People really don't understand the power of effective and productive communication. They also don't understand the damage ineffective and non productive communication can cause.

My mother was an English teacher for forty-seven years and taught three generations of students. She even taught me in my second and third grades and gave me no special treatment. My dad had to sign my homework and tests. She even kept me after school when I acted up and made me write on the chalkboard. Needless to say, I had to pay attention in class. I'm not saying this because of who she was in connection to me, but my mother was an excellent English teacher. I learned how to structure a sentence and put my words together to convey my thoughts and what I was trying to say succinctly. She laid a very important foundation I built upon when I joined the debate club in high school. The combination of the two showed me how powerful communication can be.

Over the years, I became an avid listener, one of the most important components of communication. I was always aware of the words I used. I nurtured a LCD form of communication (Least Common Denominator), where words left no gray areas. I strive to make sure my choice of words paint a clear picture for a person's mental eye to see. I absolutely *love* analogies!

But enough about me.

I am noticing more and more that people really don't care what they say or how they say it anymore. With a false sense of self-privilege and self-entitlement, people believe that they can say and do whatever they want with little to no consequences. Our focus has become getting our point across. We could care less what the other person's perspective is nor do we really listen to what someone else is trying to say. A well-known quote says, "The biggest communication problem is we do not listen to understand. We listen to reply."

Our tongues do more damage than any weapon man can create. Proverbs 12:18 (NIV) says, "The words of the reckless pierce like swords, but the tongue of the wise brings healing." The scary thing is we aren't aware of the damage we're causing to friends, loved ones, spouses, family, random persons that cross our paths on a daily basis. We use words, unaware of their meaning. We say words oblivious to the gravity of their use. We often forget that words cannot be taken back...ever! Just take a look around and listen. It will become even clearer how our world has gotten to where it is today.

One thing I am learning is that assessing a person's communication language is key to effective communication. I've learned that some people I have to talk to face-to-face because to write anything is asking for trouble. They're going to "interpret" or "read into" anything I write regardless of my choice of words. I have to ask clarification from Some people before I respond. They simply place the expectation of effective communication on the other person. They don't even care anymore until they're on the receiving end of communication coming from someone who doesn't care or thinks they're better than everyone else. Bottom line, I can't wait for the other person to do what's necessary to make sure our conversation is as productive as possible. It's on me. Today, I strive to govern what I say and how I say it even more because the alternative is to join the masses, and there is more than enough damaging communication in the world. In order to see change, I must be the change.

Have a blessed day on and in purpose!

CHAPTER 61

A person is only as good as the people
they allow in their space.

Getting through life alone means you will have never truly lived. We do nothing on our own. In some way shape or form, through six degrees of separation, someone or something helped us do everything we've done (We can debate this later, just follow me for a few tics please). A wise person understands that any successful person has a strong team around them, advising, suggesting, accepting delegated responsibilities, correcting when necessary or as the young folks say these days, "Keeping it 100!"

I say this to say that I am thankful for the team God put in my life. There is an empowering feeling when you know you have people in your corner that want nothing but the best for you with no ulterior motives or hidden agendas. We can hold one another responsible and accountable in love, mercy, and grace, following the footsteps and blueprint given to us by our Creator. Even more so, as I travel down this spiritual path, this journey is *completely* unfamiliar to me because this is the first time in my life that I'm traveling down this road on purpose. I find it important to have deep relationships with people we're trying to get to heaven together.

Last night, I was struggling with some things I did not feel were right in my church. The main misconception about this walk is that the moment you say the C word, it can do no wrong. Wrong! The church is nothing but a plethora of imperfect folks trying to follow a perfect God as best they can. We are ragged and it's only because of Him we even have the minimal hope of gaining salvation. At the end of the day, we are all human. The C word does *not* change that.

There will be times when we have differences of opinion, perception, and thoughts. That's okay! As long as we rely on His word and get the definitive answer, that's what really matters. But I digress. During this struggling time, I reached out to two brothers I have a strong relationship with, what we call a discipling relationship. These are brothers that I am completely open and transparent with, they know everything that is going on in my life and can hold me accountable as I strive to attain spiritual maturity. We were able to discuss what I was feeling, why I was feeling it, and how to gain understanding of what I'm feeling and making ensure that it's in line with what God wants of my life. I don't even want to think of what would have happened or what I would think now if I tried to do that with just my own understanding.

Isolation is one of the most powerful tools of God's adversary. I am learning that no matter how much I may feel inferior, no matter how big a mistake I've made, and no matter how wretched I am, I am not alone. We are all out here *struggling!* My struggle may not be the same as someone else's, but we're all struggling nonetheless. When we confess our struggles, confess what demons we're fighting, and strive to do better and be better, a huge weight is lifted off our shoulders. We can move forward with one less thing to face. There is a freedom in being open, there is fresh air in knowing that there are genuine people in your life who know what you're dealing with, that check on you and make sure you're good, and that pray with you and for you on a regular basis. It's amazing, and those who choose to stay hidden and isolated will never experience that and hear me when I say that to choose that path is to truly miss out on a supreme blessing in life. We're being forged into a mighty weapon, whether you choose to accept the responsibility or not. We were never meant to go through it alone. Know that you don't have to!

Today I am thankful that I am not going through life alone. I pray the very same for you.

Have a blessed day on and in purpose!

CHAPTER 62

The phrase "This is going to hurt me more than it hurts you" hits differently (no pun intended) when you're the one saying it versus being the one hearing it.

When my parents would say that before proceeding to tear the fur off my back side for any offense I committed, I would look at them thinking, *What have you been drinking? You're about to inflict physical damage to my body for what felt like an extended period of time and you're the one who's hurt? Go have a seat of the several persuasion!* I remember the first time I had to discipline my son. It was at that exact moment that I knew EXACTLY what my parents had been saying to me all those years. I called them immediately after, crying like I got the spanking myself and apologized to both of them. I told them that I get it. Boy, do it get it!

Some things are a necessary evil. Sometimes we build things up and sometimes it's most advantageous to tear things down. There are moments when you have to take several steps backward to create room to build momentum to get over an obstacle that be's (yeah I said it) in your path. There will come a time when you have to tell someone their breath stinks, knowing that it may hurt that person for that minute or two but then they may rectify their situation immediately thereafter. See...there's this thing called Godly sorrow. Never mind. That's too much for a Tuesday morning. I'm saying this to say that there are situations in life that suck, no matter which side of it you're on. There are circumstances that present no easy path to a resolution. There are times when I had to something I don't want to do. I like things that are simple, quiet, and peaceful, the opposite of conflict.

But Jesus said, "Let not my will, but your will be done" (Luke 22:42). I find some comfort in knowing that even Jesus, in His human existence, was like, "I don't want to do this! Please don't make me do this! Bump this, I'm out!" I also find it comforting that after he got His fears out, the Spirit took over immediately. He pulled himself together and got back on track, realizing that it's not about what He wants, but it's about the will of His Father. That's why He was there, why He was serving, and why He laid down His life as a sacrifice so that centuries later, I could sit here and say, "I don't want to do this today, but it's not my will but yours be done." It's also why Jesus says, "This is going to hurt me more than it hurts you." Let that marinate for a minute.

Today I take the sunshine with the rain, the bitter with the sweet. Today is my Sour Patch Kids commercial. I know that this is not where I will stay but where my lesson will be taught.

Have a blessed day on and in purpose!

CHAPTER 63

The world is very sick.

Our country is showing us why you don't put a businessman in the most powerful political position. We are killing ourselves off on a daily basis but get upset when someone of a different color than us do the same. We can stand in line for a chicken sandwich but not exercise our right to vote. We are the most sensitive society that ever existed in history. The family infrastructure is nonexistent. Knowledge and wisdom is no longer passed down from generation to generation. We have *false* sense of entitlement and refuse to be wrong. We will watch the most negative and degrading shows and listen to the most self-disrespecting music they can create and then wonder why behaviors reflect art. These things aren't even scratching the surface, and some wonder why the world is the way it is.

Every time I read a post or listen to the news, every time I see a nine-year-old girl twerking at the bus stop, every time I have to listen to a young man walking down the street and yelling out the most profane of lyrics, every time I get cut off by someone who thinks they can just get into my lane, and every time I see a child talk back disrespectfully to their parent, all I can do is ask why. I no longer waste time asking. These things are simply years of systemic programming. It should come as no shock in the times we are living in. The scripture in 2 Timothy 3:1–9 has been made manifest in ways that we can't even fathom. It does not justify the behaviors we have to endure and the dangers we now face on a daily basis, but it relieves me of trying to figure it all out. It also creates a sense of urgency since this world is going somewhere I do not wish to be.

The time I spent trying to figure out a cure is now invested in making sure that my salvation is solidified, that my family is good, and that we are aware the world is passing away. I focus on making sure that I will see my mother again in heaven. I can't change the world but I can change how I live in it. I can change my actions, my responses, my decisions. I can only control myself, knowing how this world will only get worse. It gives me a blueprint so that I can now defensively exist in it. It also gives me a peace of mind I didn't think possible in the chaos that we call civilization. I stop asking sick people a well question and expect a well answer.

Have a blessed day on and in purpose!

CHAPTER 64

Why is there someone with a background in psychology on any team that creates the application process for most Fortune 500 companies? That same person is on most teams for marketing as well. Why? It's just a commercial, right? You're just trying to get a job, right?

If you understand how something thinks, you can control that very thing. There are billions of people on this earth but only five major personality traits. Figure out a person's personality and you pretty much know who they are at their core. Businesses have perfected the use of this information for centuries. Many don't even realize they're being manipulated. Everyone has to have the latest iPhone when phones have a 2- or 3-year life span. People just have to get the newest model car when anything made after 2014 will pretty much last you years as long as you keep up with the basic maintenance. They got to have that six-bed, five-bath mansion in the suburbs when it's just them and their significant other living there. We are programmed to believe that these things bring us happiness when in reality, all they do is add stress. They don't care. They just sit back and count your money.

There's someone else who has perfected this process. He is trying to gain much more than your money. He has been here since the beginning of time. He has destroyed civilizations, taken countless lives, and now roams the earth as a roaring lion seeking to devour someone. Now he may not be able to read your mind (did you know the devil can't read your mind? We'll circle back 2205 around to that), but he most definitely take notes of people's actions. How a person governs their day-to-day activities speaks volumes of what they think and what they really want in life.

"Inception" plant the seed and that thought then becomes the man…it makes the man who they will become to be. That is a dangerously powerful concept and yet so true. Once a man sets his mind on something, it then infects the heart. Then there's pretty much nothing you can do to sway that person from the task they have set themselves to accomplish. People have absolutely no clue how *powerful* the subconscious mind is! People are living their lives as a casualty of a war that they're not even aware of. People spend their entire lives trying to acquire riches and possessions. Then they leave this earth and then what? Matthew 16:26 (NIV) reads, "What good will it be for someone to gain the whole world, yet forfeit their soul? Or what can anyone give in exchange for their soul?" But I love how it reads in the Message version (MSG), "What kind of deal is it to get everything you want but lose yourself? What could you ever trade your soul for? What is your soul worth?" Know that there are powers watching you make that determination and observing how you live.

Today I continue to make the changes in my life so that the world can see that I know what my soul is worth and that I'm trying to preserve it even more so as the end draws near.

Have a blessed day on and in purpose!

CHAPTER 65

First and foremost, special recognition to any veteran reading this post. On this day, we say thank you for your service. Many may never know the sacrifices you've made for this country, but I want to say thank you for everything you do or have done and respect to those who are no longer here because of their service. Salute!

Speaking of recognition, I just want to say that I am particularly humbled. I want to thank you all for being in my heart this morning. A little over a week ago, I posted a request of all of my Facebook friends. I asked every friend to send me a dollar through Cash App. I didn't put an explanation of what it was for. I simply made the request. Allow me to offer some insight into that request.

I have been a supporter and contributor of No-Shave November since 2013. My brother is a cancer survivor so I wanted to show my support and bring awareness to it. I pray none of us will ever have to get in the ring and go up against it. Cancer is no joke. If you know a survivor or lost someone to it, I need not go into details. In July 2016, I lost my mother. A month later, I lost her mother, my grandmother, to the exact same type of cancer. I literally watched both of them go through one of the most painful transitions. There is a much deeper story behind this, but for time sake, I will stay on the topic at hand. *Rest in heaven, Edna Wills and Helen Parran. I love you more than words can ever express.*

After they passed away, I stopped cutting my hair and went through somewhat of a Nebuchadnezzar phase, which lasted about two years. Most people didn't even notice because I always wore hats in public. It was part of my grieving but also a tribute to my brother, mother, and grandmother. I promised them I would never shave my beard ever again. I cut my hair and trimmed the beard, but I vowed to never go beardless again, and I haven't. Movember holds a special meaning to me. I am an avid supporter now more than ever.

I have close to two thousand friends in Facebook. If every friend were to give a dollar, what a wonderful donation that would be at the end of the month. I normally contribute to St. Jude Children's Hospital as they are an advocate in the fight against cancer. They do amazing work with the children who have to fight this uncaring illness. Here's where I got choked up. I honestly didn't expect *anyone* to respond. I figured I'd get some memes or a few GIFs, but that would be it. So many people abuse asking for money through Cash App. I figured people would put me in the same category. Who would I be to blame them? That's society, right? Then my phone went off. It went off again and again and again. The crazy thing is, the majority of the donations said in the notes, "Just because you asked." Sitting in the barbershop, I was tearing up. People were looking at like I've lost it. It was overwhelming to have support from people support who don't even know what they're supporting but were willing to give anyway. That is amazing but also humbling. I was trying to get through life like everybody else. The donations kept coming in. When I shared that the money would be donated to St. Jude, even more donations came in. Some people even sent five dollars and one person even sent twenty. Each time my phone went off, it was just confirmation that I'm finally getting something right.

Today I am realizing that people notice what you do and your heart behind it. I just want to inspire the same way that I've been inspired. I want to give just as I've been given. I what to spread love and joy the same way the love and joy has been extended to me. At the end of the day, we're all fighting the same fight. We're all struggling to overcome something. Every last one of us is striving to win the race. None of us are alone in what we're going through. If sharing my life and opening the door to my experiences helps someone else see that they're not alone and in some way help them to take that next step they thought they didn't have the strength to, then amen!

Amen to you all for strengthening me and encouraging me. God's plan is perfect. That means that you all being in my space is kismet. You guys have given me renewed strength, fortified humility, and encouragement to keep doing what I do. To all those who donated, to those who keep encouraging me to write a book what I do 2284 here (Believe me when I say that I'm researching it out so that I can begin), and to everyone who shared how these messages help them, know that you all are helping me. Thank you, thank you, and thank you! To God be the glory!

Have a blessed day on and in purpose!

CHAPTER 66

*The epiphany is simply the thought
that leads to the journey.*

I don't have the great idea to enter a marathon and then do nothing. Yet for far too long, that's how I've chosen to live my life. I will have a grand thought, a revelation with little to no follow through. I've said, "I'm gonna enter a marathon" and then sit back down, watch TV, and relax until the day of the marathon. Then I wonder why I can't breathe thirty steps past the starting line.

Don't act like it's just me people. A house cannot be successfully built without a blueprint. Preparation and resources are needed to achieve the desired result. I have to have a game plan, but then I have to implement and follow through with that game plan. I have to stick to the plan!

It's no easy thing to step out of one's comfort zone, yet it's only when that takes place that I truly learn to let go and let God. The thing that I must keep in mind is that this preparation isn't so that I can cross the finish line, but so that I can confidently stand at the starting line. Much like training doesn't necessarily guarantee me the win, it ensures that I will be ready for the fight. Life is the greatest fight we'll ever experience. I call it the beautiful struggle. In order to even have a chance of coming out victorious, I have to train mentally, emotionally, physically, and. most important, spiritually.

There's a war going on, whether I choose to believe in it or not. Women trafficking, selling of organs, advancement of technology beyond our comprehension—even though I don't see it, doesn't mean it's not taking place. There's an undertow that many are unaware of, but that doesn't mean I can't get pulled under by it. As much as I am preparing my mind and my body, I also need to prepare my soul. Truly it's not a sprint, it is a marathon. Today I accept that my race, my journey has just begun. On your mark...get set... GO!

Have a blessed day on and in purpose!

CHAPTER 67

I was having some very serious spiritual thoughts this morning. If that's not your thing, then you've been warned that this one may not be for you. The problem is, I create gray areas in black-and-white situations.

I was once arrested for driving on a suspended license. Because of the time that they locked me up, I ended up spending the night waiting for a commissioner to come in. There I was in a holding cell with a drug dealer, a gentleman who got pulled over and found out that there was a FTA (failure to appear) bench warrant out on him, a murderer who was on the run and got caught, a man who was drunk and got into a physical altercation outside of a club, and another who was in for domestic abuse and broke his baby momma's nose. I just had a suspended license surrounded by men who did way more than me. Why was I there? But at the end of the day, we all committed a crime. We all broke the law! Now I can look at it as my evil was the lesser of all the evils that cell that night, but it still had equal results. It still came with the same consequences.

When I read scriptures like 1 Corinthians 6:9–11 and Galatians 5:19–21, I find myself reading about some serious acts that if I willingly and continuously engage in them, they pretty much guarantee that I will lose all hope of salvation and lose my inheritance to God's kingdom. Then I read Proverbs 6:16–19. Now these may not be considered as heavy as the latter scriptures, but these are things that the Lord *hates*! They carry the same consequences as the other "heavier charges." Just like I found myself in a jail cell with murderers, abusers, and drug dealers, and all I did was drive on a suspended license. I can find myself in hell right next to murderers, fornicators, and the like for having a lying tongue. Bottom line, we all sinned. We all broke God's law!

I can only speak for myself, much like I can only focus on what I choose to believe and how I now choose to govern my life. These are my thoughts that I'm expressing, but I have to stop telling myself that because what I'm doing is a lesser offense. It's okay to commit it. As long as the rooms that visitors see are presentable, I don't need to clean the whole house. As long as I'm not killing or selling drugs, it's okay if I drive on a suspended license because I need to get to work, right? I can justify anything in my mind, but that doesn't excuse me from breaking the law.

Today my thoughts remind me that I need to get all of my affairs in order, that I need to clean my whole house, and that I need to resolve the issue with my license so I can drive with a clean conscious. I've got to get my entire life together. Otherwise, what am I living for? It's not easy. Every day I get up, I struggle. I am nothing but a sinful wretch without God. I've lived a life that clearly shows me with no equivocation who I am without God. I *never* want to be that person again. That's forty years of behaviors that I now have to uninstall, deprogram, and replace with new software. Any techie persons out there who have had to uninstall software to install a new version know that it's not a quick process. Every piece of software and whatever it has touched during the time it was operating in your system has to be removed before the new software can be installed or it may cause issues with the new installation.

Y'all missed that but it's okay.

Part of my journey is striving to become a better me, which means facing myself realistically, openly, and honestl, with no holds barred. A sober look at who I am without Him has no other rational end result but to show me clearly how much I need Him and how much I am in dire need of the His mercy and forgiveness. Even more so, I need the love, the wisdom, the power, and the grace He extends to me that I will never be worthy to receive.

I have to stop living my life as if gray areas will get me into heaven. It all has consequences, good or bad. You get one call when you're locked up so it would be in your best interest to make that call count. You call that one person you *know* will help you out in your time of need, one person you can depend on without a doubt. Today I will continue with even more conviction to call on God.

Have a blessed day on and in purpose!

CHAPTER 68

I can't live my life for you.

I have the right to make decisions in my life as I see fit. I am blessed with this thing called my own opinion that does have to match anyone else's and feelings that do not have to be judged by any outside persons, places, or things. What I do, how I live, and the path I am called to travel on will not always make sense to those on the outside looking in. I am okay with that. Today's society is so judgmental. But when the light is shined on those who judge us, we're told we need to be more understanding. There is only one judgment I am concerned with, and it does not belong to any person who dwells on this earth.

Should I take into consideration the feelings and opinions of others, especially those close to me? Of course! To isolate myself and make a decision based on my level of understanding. When I have family and friends that I interact with on a regular basis and who may be affected by my decisions, it is absolutely ridiculous. I'm not saying that I do not care what other people think or how they feel as it pertains to the decisions that I am making. But there are times when my decision will not make sense to others but me. It's at that time that I cannot concern myself with what others may think or say when I know what's best for me. My path is for me to walk on, for me to comprehend, and for me to receive the blessings that come with it. It is *not* for everybody and thank God that that statement is fact.

Wisdom and discernment is necessary to know when to do which. There are times when a person must stand their ground even if no one will stand with them. Some of you are trying to live someone else's life now and are failing miserably because you simply refuse to live the life that's meant for you. I pray that your eyes will be opened to the reality. No matter how bad it may seem to you, it is your life and no one else's. That is a blessing that very few people understand and accept.

I accept my life and all that comes with. If someone can't understand that, then it's okay. I will be okay.

Have a blessed day on and in purpose!

CHAPTER 69

He, the devil, will always attack you at your weakest point, he will without hesitation use the very thing you are most sensitive to. He will use anything and anyone to accomplish your destruction. He spares no expense, and there are no holds barred. He will not stop until he brings you to your knees. I read 1 Corinthians 10:13.

God has prepared me for everything I will go through. He has given me the victory over everything I will encounter on my journey—the joys and the pains, ups and the downs, highs and lows, and successes and failures. But here's something that I had to embrace recently. His victory will not stop you from experiencing the pain that comes from the devil's attacks! Jesus had the greatest victory as a human in the history of mankind. He successfully sacrificed His perfect life in exchange for our sins. As His birth is celebrated during this time of the year, we reflect on the significance of His death. But that victory came a great cost. The pain He endured to accomplish that victory should forever touch our hearts and remind us never to give up because if He could go through that, we literally have no excuse. None!

This path does not exclude me from pain, heartache, and failures. It does not shield me from the feelings associated with those experiences. But I know God's plan is perfect and His will be done. If His will is to provide me a means of escape from any of the devils attempts to thwart my salvation, then my faith should rest comfortably in that undeniable fact. We may not always understand why and

I'm learning even more so that it's not my job to understand why, it's my job to have faith in the God I serve. As long as He knows, then I'm in good hands and my faith will not go without results.

If you are dealing with the loss of a loved one, know that you are not alone. You are now a member of a very exclusive club that only those who have joined know about. God's plan is perfect. In His infinite wisdom, gave you yet another incentive to get to know Him and get to heaven so that you can see your loved ones again. I believe that wholeheartedly that it has started a fire in me that will not be put out ever until I see my family again. Then we can all laugh and cry together.

Have a blessed day all and know that you are already victorious. To God be the glory!

CHAPTER 70

*Sometimes things happen so you
can see where your heart is.*

Just because your heart is in the right place does not mean that it will be matched by those around you or those you serve. That should *not* stop you from serving or change your heart about serving.

If I'm at a light and someone is at the light asking for spare change, I have no problem giving what I have or giving them something. What they do with what I give them is something they will have to render an account for. I am accountable to serve and that's what I will be held to. Do people say they're homeless when they're not? Yes. Say they hungry when they know they're going to use the money for drugs? Yes. Should any of that keep me from doing what I am admonished as a Christian should do? No.

According to Luke 6:38 (NIV), "Give, and it will be given to you. A good measure, pressed down, shaken together and running over, will be poured into your lap. For with the measure you use, it will be measured to you." There is more joy in giving than receiving, which is why God gave His only begotten Son for us sinners. He knew most of us would not use that gift for what He intended it for, but He gave anyway. He knew the majority would reject His gift, but He did it anyway, setting the standard for the measure in which we should give. We shouldn't focus on what we can get in return, but rather to give because that's what we're supposed to do, period. How we choose to give shows us where our heart is. That should be a cause for reflection and adjustment if necessary.

Have a blessed day on and ins purpose!

CHAPTER 71

Let me preface this by saying that what I'm about to share is my conviction and beliefs. If you do not agree, that's what's makes the country the great place it is. With that being said.

For me, the Bible is the standard. If we are to have a spiritually based discussion, the majority of your points should be found therein, not in a side publication, not a plethora of theological quotes from a scholar (unless directly supported by scripture), or just how a person feels because that's all they know. The moment you cannot support your statements via scripture, those statements immediately become opinion to me. I have the right to agree or disagree with someone's opinion.

Acts 17:11 (NIV, emphasis added) says, "Now the Berean Jews were of more noble character than those in Thessalonica, for they received the message with great eagerness and *examined* the Scriptures every day to see if what Paul said was true." Here, Apostle Paul, who walked and served with Jesus, spoke to the Bereans. His reputation wasn't enough, his mere words weren't enough. They still examined the scriptures to make sure that what he said was true. That's how we should be.

The sad truth is that there are so many persons who have built their faith in words spoken and never took the time to see if those words were true. If that's how you choose to live your life, if that has led to you having a personal and intimate relationship with God, then amen. Please do not expect me to just follow along with your ideologies as you read them out of a book that is not scripture, especially if when I ask you to offer scriptural support and you're unable to or you have to research it and get back to me. It's not enough. With a Berean's heart, it's no longer acceptable.

I am not claiming to be perfect or that I know it all, but I know enough to know that everything I need to know is in His word. Once the standard has been set, then anything someone is trying to convince me of must be proven within its content. I may have been born at night, but I wasn't LAST NIGHT!

Have a blessed day on and in purpose!

CHAPTER 72

When the Spirit says move. move! DUH!

It amazes me that I can take full assurance that I can breath but be hesitant that God will take care of me if I put my faith in Him. I have more confidence that my car will start in the morning than the fact that God has already made me victorious over this world and it's ruler. I can take full assurance that I can breath but am still hesitant that God will take care of me if I put my faith in Him, which leads me to one simple conclusion… I don't know jack!

I consider myself a very intelligent person. I've lived a lot in this short time that I've been here, but I've learned a lot in the process. Having all that information, I still find myself struggling with the concept of letting God be God and moving in His wisdom and by His spirit. I still find myself asking, "Are you sure?" Whenever He gives me instructions, I ask, "Is there another way I can do that? Can I take the path of least resistance?" To question the Creator of all things, I have to smack myself on a regular basis. He is omnipotent, the Alpha and Omega. He created me. Why am I questioning His decisions? It just confirms my imperfect makeup and my need to draw closer to Him even more. The fall back and let your friend catch you theory to the 100th power, but who better to catch me?

First Corinthians 10:13 has become my second mantra, which helps me accomplish my first motto in Matthew 6:33. I pray for less of me and more of God.

Have a blessed day on and in purpose!

CHAPTER 73

*The easiest way to keep a person down is to
never allow them the opportunity to rise.*

Watching a lion hunt is fascinating and has kept me glued to the TV for hours. It's an art and something they perfect because at the end of the day, this is how they eat and stay alive. It's not their strength that makes them king of the jungle because there are many animals that are far stronger than a lion. It's the fact that they're one of the wisest animals in the jungle. They think through and implement actions based on the experience they've gained, the very definition of wisdom. When they hunt, they go for the easy prey—the young, the weak, and those not paying attention. This guarantees survival. These provide food for their pride, their family. It's not that they can't take down the leader, but they work hard and efficiently.

Where am I going with this? Glad that you asked. There is a lion roaming this earth and seeking to devour someone (1 Pet. 5:8). Although he is extremely strong, it's not his strength that many had fallen prey to his evil ways. It's his cunning implementation of centuries of experience. Using his craft to guarantee the fall of many. This lion goes after the easy prey, the young, the weak, those not paying attention. He's not worried about feeding the pride. He wants to ensure that our souls cannot be saved. This lion plays for far higher stakes. The price his prey pays is higher than just their lives. Knowing that this lion exists and is roaming the earth freely, I do what is necessary to stay on guard and prepare for his attacks. One of the things you will notice when a lion hunt is the first priority is to keep his prey down. He knows that if his victim gets back up, there's a chance that they can get away and survive. The more his prey tries to get away, the more pressure he applies to bite down. His grip gets to guarantee that no escape is possible. It's not until you put up a fight that he puts forth an effort to keep you down.

You missed that, but it's okay, you'll get it later.

No, I kind of need you to get this now.

You ever notice how when you determine that things need to change in your life, or you decide to take a leap of faith, or discover your calling and begin making preparations to pursue it, that that's when all Hades breaks loose? This start coming out of the wood works things start happening that normally would never take place obstacles form that don't even make sense and yet they appear and now you're faced with them. The first inclination is to give up, to go back to business as usual, to try again at another time. If you've ever experienced that in any way, you know what it feels like when the lion roaming this earth applies pressure to keep you down. He knows that a way to was made for you to get up, get out, and get to where you've been called to be. He knows that if you get up, you'll get away and your soul will be saved so he does all he can to keep you down. Most tire out and give up. That's what he expects you to do. But if you're an avid *Wild Kingdom* viewer like me, (Yeah, I know… time stamp…and I SO DON'T CARE! LOL!) you know that there are those who don't give up. They take a deep breath, dig deep, and continue to fight, kicking and screaming. It may take a while and may look like the battle is lost. Then out of nowhere, they break free from the deadly grip of the lion.

Escape is possible. A way has been made. you can survive. you just can't give up. you have to stay strong. take a deep breath, dig deep, and keep on fighting. But, we can't do it alone…trying to do it by ourselves is a complete recipe for staying in the grip of he who is devouring many. It begins with knowledge of God, Knowledge of God leads to knowledge of self, and it's in that combination that our convictions, faith, love, and strength reside. When you dig deep, that means you're planting yourself in something, taking root, fortifying your position. If there is nothing to dig deep into, what are you going to do? Some potential prey the lion looks goes after for a later time (they don't stay off the radar forever). They are constantly on guard. They prepared and gird themselves physically, mentally, emotionally, and spiritually.

It's not enough for me to walk around saying Jesus is Lord with a roaring lion seeking to devour me. I have to be ready. I have to be prepared, I have to be connected. I have to dig deep and fortify myself in His word. I have to strengthen myself physically, mentally, emotionally, and spiritually. I have to strive to be the best me so that I will be ready when it comes time to go up against an adversary that has centuries to perfect his attack.

Food for thought, in the 70's, there was a show called *Happy Days* in the seventies that was almost taken off the air because one of the characters said the word *hell*. Now a character can drop the F-bomb on prime time and no one even flinches. This kind of desensitization you can't even determine when and where the shift took place. It's just a small sample of the level of chess playing this lion is utilizing to destroy the world. When you look around and observe everything going on in the world, you quickly see that man is not in control of this earth. It's truly in the power of the wicked one. Trump is the *least* of your worries. All he can do is take all our money and send us to war. I'm more worried about the lion that comes between me and my salvation, knowing that the greatest trick he ever played was convincing the world he doesn't exist.

Today I accept that it's up to me to prepare for the ongoing fight for my salvation. Whatever it takes, whatever I need to do, whatever changes in my life need to be made; whatever training of my mind, body, and soul need to do; and whatever persons, places, and things in or out of my life, it needs to happen *right now*! Today when I see the lion, and when you decide to come this way, I will be ready.

Have a blessed day on and in purpose!

CHAPTER 74

*Please forgive me, my thoughts are all over
the place this morning, but here it goes.
There's a freedom that exists outside of one's comfort
zone that unfortunately many will never discover.*

There are people who go to the same restaurant on the same night at the same time, wearing the same clothes. They're seated by the same hostess at the same booth with the same plates and utensils. They order the same food off the same menu cooked by the same chef. Tonight they expect the food to taste different.

Yeah, I'm the same way, normally with the same results. Good or bad, I knew what the end result would be so there were no surprises. I knew how the relationship was going to turn out so I may not be happy, but I won't get hurt. I was going nowhere, but I knew where nowhere was and what was taking place in nowhere so I was okay with nowhere. Sounds crazy, doesn't it? Yet, that's the majority of people's existence in this day and age.

Comfort zone is a place or situation where one feels safe or at ease and without stress. Life is so simple these days. We live in a society where technically you never have to leave your house and can survive effectively. People even work from home now. There's nothing you can't order that won't be at your front door in minutes. You have remote controls to everything. A person never have to get up to have access to everything they need for that day. This has also lead to bad health, increased inactivity, lethargy, lack of social skills, depression, and the list goes on and on. Once a person gets comfortable, it becomes very difficult to change those habits. Habits are hard to break, whether they're productive or destructive. Most opt to just continue in their current existence because it's easier to deal with their norm, regardless of what that norm looks like.

Sooner or later, there comes the need for change. Depending on how long a person has been "comfortable," it can be extremely difficult to achieve the desired change. For most, the difficulty or fear lies in the unknown. The next step isn't clear. The direction or the outcome is not guaranteed. There's risks in the unknown, uncertainty, and potential for failure and regret, but there's freedom in faith. That's what most people overlook and never see because they rarely become fully invested in the concept. They dip their toe in the pool and quickly pull it back because the water is too cold. If you're a cannonballer like myself, that water is crazy cold. However, you can adjust quickly and continue to swim in the water. It's called a *leap of faith* for a reason.

Today I embrace the freedom in the unknown because there are things I do know that overshadow my fear and uncertainties. It's called faith. I'm learning more and more about its blessings as I'm allowed each day to live. My prayer is that you learn about its blessings as well.

Have a blessed day on and in purpose!

You can learn a lesson in any situation.

Occasionally I go to the Dunkin Donuts on my way in to work; grab me a caramel iced coffee and a sesame seed bagel toasted with butter; to start my eight-hour workday. Today as I was leaving the store, the following conversation took place with a young man standing outside:

> *Him: Big bro, can you help me out?*
> *Me: Excuse me?*
> *Him: I'm saying, can you help me out?*
> *Me: With what?*
> *Him: They told me to ask so I'm asking.*
> *Me: What are you asking? I don't understand the question.*
> *Him: I'm saying if I had it, I wouldn't be out here asking, but I'm asking if you can help me out.*
> *Me: Young man, let's start over. What is it that you are asking for? Don't assume I know what you're talking about. Ask as if I have no idea what you're talking about because in this instance, that would be the exact case.*
> *Him: I'm sorry, man. Can I have a dollar or some change so I can get something to eat?*

Me: We can go in here and I can get you something to eat if you'd like.

Him: Naw, man, I'm good.

Me: Then what were you really asking for?

Him: I'm saying, I'm just trying to get some help.

Me: What kind of help are you trying to get? You said you wanted some money to get something to eat. I offered to get you something to eat. That wasn't good enough for you. So what kind of help are you really asking for?

Him: You don't understand, man.

Me: Young man, I've been homeless and I've been broke so I do understand. I understand that you have to be at a certain point in your life to stand outside of an establishment and ask people for money for whatever reason. I need you to understand that you're making that request from people who are working hard every day to have the money they give you. If you're going to ask that of them, then there is a manner, a way, and a heart you need to have when you ask. No one is interested in giving their money away. Even a person with a giving heart becomes hesitant when the person asking comes with questionable intent. So you can't say that you want something to eat and then someone offers to get you something to eat but you reject the very thing you asked for. How do you think that looks to the person reaching for their pocket to give away money they didn't plan on spending. I'm about to spend my lunch money so that you can get something to eat. Just because I'm about to give you food instead of money, you have an issue? How do you think that looks to me, the person you're asking to help you out?

Him: You right, big bro. Can I get something to eat please?

I took him inside and got him some food. I also gave him some numbers that I keep in my wallet if he truly wanted help. I told him where my church was where he was more than welcome to visit. I also talked to him about his sales pitch and how it could go over a lot better with some minor adjustments. Outside the store, I asked if I could pray with him. To which he said yes. After we prayed, I wished him well. As I got in my car, I was immediately humbled. I went back and gave him the change from the food I ordered. He had a perplexed look on his face. He was like, "That's your lunch money, right?" I said, "Yes, but you taught me a valuable lesson today. Here, take this, and God bless you." I shook his hand and got back in my car. How he asked me for help is often how I ask God for help. I'm not clear and have ulterior motives behind what I'm asking for. I assume God knows what I'm asking for and will just give it to me because I'm asking. As soon as He offers me something else, I don't want it even though I need it. This young man made me look at myself and pray forgiveness at 6:57a.m. God put that young man in my space today so that I could be a blessing to him and so he could be a blessing to me in turn. It never ceases to amaze me how God works in my life. When I look at things the right way, I can see just how He's working.

Today I'm learning that we are all human. Walking past those who less fortunate is a disservice to the blessing that may be in store for us in. God serves us even though we're not worthy of Him. I work hard for the little money I have, but when I look at what I have in my possession, my money didn't buy any of that. God's grace blessed me with it so I can of service and a blessing to others. I don't have a lot, but I give because I've been given.

Be a blessing to someone because you are blessed beyond measure.

Have a blessed day on and in purpose!

CHAPTER 76

*It all begins with knowledge of self. If
I don't know myself, how will anyone
else be able to get to know me?*

Let me preface this by saying that the views expressed by one Christopher Wills are his and his alone and do not reflect the views of anyone else. With that being said, I present to you the crayon box theory.

I believe every person is like a basic set of eight colors: brown, red, yellow, purple, black, orange, green, and blue. Now we could spend a class session breaking down what each color represents, but for today's argument, let's keep things high end, okay?

With the premise that none of us are perfect, let's say, for argument's sake, that each individual is missing two crayons. A person is not going to know which two are missing. This means that a person would have to examine themselves to determine which crayons are missing. That information is critical in knowing where a person is lacking. A better way of looking at it is knowing what they need. This is especially critical when looking for a mate and or better half. If a person is unaware of what they need, how does the search even begin? How do I know what I'm looking for if I haven't taken the time to identify what is actually lost? Is it realistic for me to think that my quest will be successful if I don't even have the slightest idea what it is I'm looking for? It could potentially be right in front of my face and I wouldn't know it because I am unaware that that's even what I need. Doesn't that sound confusing? That confusion is what I see when people talk to me about their relationships or their search for it. People are unaware of the crayons they're missing, trying to find crayons in someone else. If I don't know what colors I'm missing, how can I possibly find a person who fills what I'm lacking? How would I appreciate them fully if I don't know that what they're bringing to the table is in fact what I really need? How do I know that I'm good for someone else when I don't truly know what I'm bringing to the table? If we're both missing the same colors, how are we ever going to benefit one another?

Just think how specific my search becomes when I am clear about what it is that I'm looking for. Certain persons, places, and things I now by pass because I know that looking there isn't necessary to find what it is I'm seeking. If I'm in need of Green and Yellow and a person presents Red and Blue, does it make sense to continue my search there? Will I continue to invest time and and energy knowing that they don't possess what I really need? If I do stay, can I truly blame them when I knew from the beginning they didn't have what I needed to begin with? Better question, if I do stay, can I honestly say that I knew what I needed? Even better, am I staying because I want or need something?

I can keep asking these questions for days, but it starts with knowledge of self. No one knows who they are automatically. I must decide to make that discovery for my own benefit. If I don't take the time to get to know myself, love, accept me, embrace, forgive, encourage, uplift, and rebuild myself, then I am ice skating uphill in my journey. Then I discover and learn that it's through God we truly becomes successful. He gives me the blueprint because He made me. In discovering Him, he shows what I'm missing and what I need. He aids me in discovering all that comes with me. Knowing who I am cuts down a lot of wasted time in my life. Knowing what I need and, more importantly, what I *don't* need cuts out so much nonsense in my life. Things I used to entertain or absolute NO's on my timeline. People I used to be around are no longer there because they were only there for what I wanted. Now I know what I need. Major difference! That went over your heads, but you'll get it later.

When you know better, you do better! Going into this world and not having knowledge of self is the equivalent of not knowing how to build a house or building your dream home by yourself with no blueprints, instructions, or guidance. Then after you put it all together and fill it with all your prized possessions, expecting a totally positive outcome, there is something else you should know. There are people out here who look for those who are unaware of who they are. They know they can be easily manipulated and used them however they may see fit. They actually look for someone who has not taking the time to discover themselves and then create a narrative for that person, convincing them the sky is actually green and water is dry. Not to mention, you got that whole lion roaming the earth thing going on, and he tricked two perfect individuals into destruction. He's a beast with his, no pun intended.

Today I am learning that life is not a game. Not taking the time to get to know myself is treating my life like it's just a game.

Have a blessed day on and in purpose!

Hello, everyone. Let me formally introduce myself. My name is Christopher Wills. I am forty-six years old, born and raised in Baltimore, Maryland. I currently work for Baltimore City Public Schools. I've been employed there for over twenty years. I'm also a professional DJ, DJ Droopy. I've been blessed to follow that passion for twenty years professionally as well. I work with a wonderful mentoring program, AZIZA PE&CE, which uses the arts to teach life skills to youth, from fourteen to twenty-four years of age.

Last but certainly not least, in fact saving the best for last, I made Jesus lord of my life on July 24, 2013. In fact, that's one of the major reasons why you're reading this right now. If not for Him, I would not have the courage to do this. To God be the glory.

I am son of God, a husband, father of two children, and friend to many. I thoroughly enjoy music and movies, and I am striving to answer my calling by writing this book and being completely in hopes that someone will no longer feel that they're the only one feeling the way they do as they go through life. I am not a scholar, professional psychologist, or any of that. I am just a man who has learned some things while living on the planet, and I just want to share my experiences with the world in hopes to encourage, uplift, give hugs, give insight, give a different perspective, and last but certainly not the least, be a light and bring glory and honor to our Lord and Savior.